GOODBYE, MEXICO:
POEMS OF
REMEMBRANCE

EDITED BY
SARAH CORTEZ

Texas Review Press
Huntsville, Texas

FIRST EDITION

Requests for permission to acknowledge material from this work should be sent to:

Permissions
Texas Review Press
English Department
Sam Houston State University
Huntsville, TX 77341-2146

Cover Design: Nancy Parsons

Library of Congress Cataloging-in-Publication Data

Goodbye, Mexico : poems of remembrance / Sarah Cortez. ~ Edition: First.
    pages cm
  ISBN 978-1-68003-004-4 (pbk. : alk. paper)
  1. American poetry~21st poetry. 2. Mexico~Poetry. 3. Mexican-American Border
Region~Poetry. I. Cortez, Sarah, editor.
  PS617.G66 2014
  811'.608035872084~dc23
                                  2014035933

This book is dedicated to the men and women of law enforcement who have already begun to give their lives in the necessary fight against narco-terrorism in the U.S.

CONTENTS

MEXICO: CRADLE OF MYTH

MEXICO: CATCH-BASIN OF DESIRE

MEXICO: ALWAYS GLISTENING

MEXICO: PRAYER BLOSSOMING A PATH

MEXICO: LABYRINTH OF LABYRINTHS

MEXICO: A BROKEN PLACE

MEXICO: CRADLE OF MYTH

A CERTAIN LIE ABOUT THE PHOENIX

It was seen in Egypt;
Certain saints swore to it:
Some sightings here and there,
Claims tenuous

Of existence storied
Not like the dragon, worm
Of heaven. No, this bird
Of fire, barely

Restrained by rainbow plumes,
Flume of fire's flight, it touched
But once in every age,
Enraged to ash.

But where? Ptolemies claimed
Its nest, but in claiming,
Proved their longing lack:
No, New World held

Its only death, fiery
Rise and flight: burning sands
And reddy rocks alone
Were burning proof.

Despite your claim, Old World,
Your tottering longing,
Glory flies from low boasts:
In Mexico, it nests.

—Seth Strickland

STORIES

Let me tell you of the eagle on the cactus,
clenching a snake in its beak. The Aztecs
claimed it as an omen, chose to build
a city there. In such a place, the roads
grow slick with legends.

And I can tell you stories of lives secluded
behind walls strung with barbed wire, dense
with ivy, where women sat, waiting for marriage,
growing their nails too long for housework.
They called them sorrow's daughters.

You don't want to hear about the dead man
who identified his killer, do you? Or the wheel chair
heaped with shattered glass? How about the family
who grew to resemble their portrait,
then sued the painter?

Here's one whispered neighbor to neighbor.
Juan Caño traded his daughter for three bottles
of tequila. Some disagree—No! For two jugs
of *pulque*—and a handgun. Memories grow dull
with use, like kitchen knives.

Of course, I could spin tales of summer droughts,
dead cattle strewn along the road, crops perished,
workers abandoning fields, factory at a standstill,
those who can, fleeing north. Some by foot.
But those you already know.

—*Diana Anhalt*

MAYA

There is dense stillness
in the ruins. Through thick

foliage small flashes
of the sky's clear light.

In the *Cenote Sagrado*
stacked skeletons, jade

and gold. On a stone
wall sacrificial markings:

the flicking
tongue of a lone iguana.

—*Kathleen Markowitz*

EL TAJÍN

The rules of this place announce themselves
on the stones surrounding the ball court.
Every wall holds stories of players
who travailed here in front of parents,
wives, neighbors, kings. Even gods
lounged in vats of *pulque* on the hillsides
watching these warriors run the field.

Their game was brutally simple—
keep a rubber ball off the ground
without hands or feet, find
space on a surface long and slender
like a serpent's back, beat
the other men with speed and desire.
Do these things and heaven opens.

The carvings show all this
in glorious tribute. They also preserve
the history of warriors who failed,
their hands held behind their backs,
their necks tilted toward the setting sun,
the knife poised close to open
its own path to heaven.

It's easy to imagine parents shining
with pride in this dying light. From above
the north court, I could see my own son
running free as he does on a soccer field
every weekend, taller and faster than the others.
His would be a fine head to offer
these gods, hair golden, eyes, blazing blue.

—*Jack B. Bedell*

THE RIGHT FOOT OF JUAN DE OÑATE

On the road to Taos, in the town of Alcalde, the bronze
        statue
of Juan de Oñate, the conquistador, kept vigil from his
        horse.
Late one night a chainsaw sliced off his right foot, stuttering
through the ball of his ankle, as Oñate's spirit scratched
and howled like a dog trapped within the bronze body.

Four centuries ago, after his cannon fire burst to burn
        hundreds
of bodies and blacken the adobe walls of the Acoma Pueblo,
Oñate wheeled on his startled horse and spoke the decree:
all Acoma males above the age of twenty-five would be
        punished
by amputation of the right foot. Spanish knives sawed
        through ankles;
Spanish hands tossed feet into piles like fish at the
        marketplace.
There was prayer and wailing in a language Oñate did
        not speak.

Now, at the airport in El Paso, across the river from Juárez,
another bronze statue of Oñate rises on a horse frozen
        in fury.
The city fathers smash champagne bottles across the
        horse's legs
to christen the statue, and Oñate's spirit remembers the
        chainsaw
carving through the ball of his ankle. The Acoma Pueblo
        still stands.
Thousands of brown feet walk across the border, the desert
of Chihuahua, the shallow places of the Río Grande, the
        bridges
from Juárez to El Paso. Oñate keeps watch, high on
        horseback
above the Río Grande, the law of the conquistador rolled
in his hand, helpless as a man with an amputated foot,

spirit scratching and howling like a dog within the bronze
body.

—*Martín Espada*

THE OLD ONES WARN OF LA LLORONA

It's always *los ancianos* who know, who confess
having seen her once part the reeds with her arms
white as fog,

having heard her howl outside their locked windows,
pressing the panes with soaked palms, rapping the glass
with her blue knuckles.

No one is safe your age, they explain. They heard
from a friend of a friend of a *chico* who slipped from his
     home
for a girl, who met a strange woman

who lured him to the river like a cat with a string.
When she finished, she hung his shed jacket
on a dead limb.

Tonight she trolls the street in her boots,
rattles the gates she passes to learn who is foolish enough
to leave one unlocked.

Who are those children asleep in their gowns
beneath windows which slide like a fish in her hands?
Who are those children? Will they come with her?

Oh, they will. Oh, they will.

—*Paul David Adkins*

7

THE RED HAND AT KABAH

Margarita Angelina Alfonso would say
that the red hand painted
on the arch at Kabah was actually painted
by one of her ancestors,

and that another one of her ancestors
painted the matching blue hand
on the other arch at Uxmal
at the end of the *sacbe*
that joined the two cities.

And she knew this, she would tell us,
because she had Mayan blood
in her veins.

It took skill to climb so high,
without rope or ladder,
to paint the colored hands she would say.
But then everyone would see—
and they would take that journey knowing
there was an ending and a beginning.

And who's to say it wasn't true?

We did know that her husband
was the most handsome man
any of us had ever seen.
He would sometimes stick feathers in her hair
and make her blush.

We also knew that when they danced together
they always knew the edge of the dance floor.
Their nostrils always flared together.
Their feet always knew exactly
when the music would stop.

—Alan Birkelbach

MEXICO CITY, 1977

I twirl the wire bookstand
in an old-fashioned drug store
crammed with magazines and medicines,
candies and plastic toys. It sits
at the intersection of two narrow streets
where for a moment, my attention
is drawn to cars and *camiones* honking.
Hands fly out windows, making questionable
gestures. Voices yell unintelligible threats.
　　　Then, there it is,
the book I've been looking for—
without knowing it, until I see the cover:
a grotesque polychrome mask
with startling white eyes, bloody
cheeks, an even bloodier tongue
sticking out between two white fangs.
Cambio de piel—A Change of Skin.
　　　From the first page,
I fall prisoner to the dark and probing
world of Carlos Fuentes. Over coffee
and churros, I watch his Mexico City
jump from the pages and surround me—
gay and grim, noisy and fierce. Foreign,
yet mesmerizing for this *norteamericana.*
Poverty and wealth, dirt and luxury,
church bells and radios blasting
an endless stream of staccato *español.*
　　　Ghosts rise from Fuentes' pen
and wrap me in the pained
exquisite. The mythic past
shudders under the city's skin,
its ancient gods, jaguars, serpents.
Though they are carved in stone, they pulse
from the book into the streets.
　　　His Mexico City becomes mine,
a place deeper than the drug store.
Though Fuentes hands me a key,
its mysteries remain forever locked.

I stand in awe at its shadowed door,
questioning its ambiguities, its struggles,
its Aztec, Mayan, Toltec deities and the one
of Catholicism. The complications of a country
where hearts, literal and figurative,
must be offered up to gods and God.

—Sandi Stromberg

AT A LUXURY RESORT

In a mini-zoo one night
a caged jaguar screams
a sound unformed by tongue,
amplified by rib bellows,
pressed through iron bars
until it shatters my tourist sleep,
brings me to the animal's side.

Once jaguars slid silently through
this jungle, spots rippling tall grass
vertical as swords. Their cries echoed
nine times in temples bearing their names,
and priests bent in fear and gratitude
offering sacrificial hearts to holy jaws.

What can I know of a caged god's needs?
The monotony of my eyes breaks his patience,
sends him in circles on *Nopalli*-sized paws
to scratch scars in gray concrete. He
bellows again from his grassless cell,
sprays, as if at any moment he might
ignite, burn in his own water, and ascend.

The hotel believes he is a charm
on our vacation bracelets, exotic
to watch as a museum piece, eyes
studded with jade. But alone
at his dark cage, far from hotel lights,
real eyes warn me away. I'm not
the one he's calling. But tonight,
I'm the one who answers, the one
who remembers to bring a heart.

—Carolyn Dahl

LA LLORONA PLAYS THE
ROLE OF AZTEC HEROINE

I dreamt Cortez sailed one of our sons
to Spain,
returned him to Mexico and my people,
once an eagle,
transformed to *el cadejo*,

hellhound unleashed
from a jeweled strap,
red teeth stripping bare
the last rib blade
of Moctezuma.

So I slipped
both my boys
into the envelope of the river,
sealed it with a signet
of moonlight,
delivered it to Xolotl's
tender hands.

I waded to the bank,
remorseless fox.

In the city, I cried *¡O mis niños!*
Every night—*¡Mis niños!*

I cried for the living
boys who teased me and
tossed stones
and burning sticks
into my gnarls of hair.

I
cried for the women
who clacked pottery shards together
to drown my approaching voice
in the black canals of their ears.

I screamed for them,
those who soon enough

would wade black rivulets
clogged with the corpses
of their own sons,

their *niñas* shredded on the cocks
and battleaxes
of conquistadors.

I cried for them all

before the altars'
toppled idols
lay shattered to shivers,

I cried, surrounded on that
dust floor stained
terra-cotta brown.

—*Paul David Adkins*

LA LLORONA AT RÍO DEL ORO

Río del Oro waxed its saddle
with midnight splash
as a woman sloshed the shallows
clutching her *niños*
still groggy in cotton gowns.

As her soles lifted
from the cold bed, she
released them
to whirl in the dark current,
their screams dragged off
in the blather of water.

On the bank, her horse
snorted, the crescent light of its
eyes a sickle sweeping.
She staggered beside
it, wringing her
hair. Frogs flopped at her
feet as she twisted the black braids dry.

She mounted and swatted
the mare with a switch
to return to her *vaquero*
empty-handed,
even as he opened the door to the town bordello.
Light flooded him,
snagged his black shadow
in the limbs of a yucca.

—*Paul David Adkins*

MEXICO: CATCH-BASIN OF DESIRE

LA LLORONA PLAYS THE ROLE
OF TREACHEROUS LA MALINCHE

Lover of Cortez,
drowner of sons,
grinding your grief
on the wheel of a nation.

You straddled your Spaniard
by the light of the burning
Templo Mayor.

Desiring heaven,
you ascended halfway
on the bodies of children.
Your wisp moans through cities
searching for more.

Malinche, he whispered,
post-coital.
He twirled your hair
with a hilt-calloused hand.

You smoothed
a smuggled map of *Tenochtitlán*,
with your long fingers,
tracing the causeways
crossing the lake
to the palaces,
gold, and the gold.

He smiled,
clutched the heft of your breast,
that astonishing jewel,
to himself.

You surrendered
everything
to him.

Your people
remember you, *Malinche*, you
weeping, you crying,
you wringing your hands
like a *guajira* at laundry.

You drowning,
you scheming, seduced
and seductress.

The bones of your sons
are your first steps to hell,

your name the black key—

Swing open
its gate.

—*Paul David Adkins*

FIRST MANGO

Veracruz, Mexico

Nineteen, and my world
was italicized. A shower curtain parted
and there it was, wet, naked.

One hot pepper and three bottles
of Coke. Dare me anything.
Carelessly sunburned and in love,

I jumped off a ten-meter board
an endless plunge through air
then water, then the rising miracle
of breath.

*

Peeled mango on a stick,
juice running down,
the pure sex of it

closed-eye bliss
over my chin,
down my neck.

I wandered lost, happily expelled
from the Garden,
delirious, all tongue.

—*Jim Daniels*

ASTRAL

for Leonora Carrington

Her soul was folklore
and her body was the shadow of alphabet
written backwards in secret code.
I will try to tell you a story:
how the lamp of her
arrived before she did, a ghost
among the masks and tapestries at market—
invisible tongue of quartz, hands like jellyfish,
mouth of inner shell. And how delicate the silver thread
that led back to the flesh-protected skull.
When she first showed up, they were
pouring the Lerma from a big jug
into cuts of land. They were stitching cities
on an old loom. She'd always known it
would take a country to decode her,
and as she removed the sutures of logic
and unbound the lyrics of her being,
she remembered it: *Mexico,*
the word she'd been dreaming all along.

—*Melissa Studdard*

POR LA LIBRE

Just out of Reynosa, you shifted into fifth
And roared to the state line, cigarette in hand.
At the checkpoint we just waved our IDs,
My license, your green card, no need for permits
Or passports then. You pulled into a *depósito*,
Bought a six-pack of Tecate Light
And then we hit the freeway. Clutching
A can between your knees, you
Worked the gearshift like a racer,
Blazing along a thin ribbon of grey
Down that arid, brush-specked plain,
Alejandra Guzmán crooning hoarse against guitars
As I leaned back in the bucket seat, watching you,
The wind snatching at your dark curls,
Rattling your earrings.

I surrendered myself to the speed, to the road,
Utterly in your hands as you blew through Río Bravo,
The towns of China and Los Ramones a distant blur,
The petroleum fields of Cadereyta belching fire—
Two hundred kilometers in about two hours.
At Guadalupe you looped to skirt Monterrey
Till the Sierra Madre rushed rocky toward us,
The massive "M" of Chipinque verdant with pine.
You downshifted, took us up that sinuous road,
Parked away from other cars. Then hand-in-hand,
Intoxicated by the drive, the music, the beer,
We slipped into those dappled shadows
Beneath the gnarled and silent boughs
And made love upon the leaves and needles
Like a Huastec couple three millennia past,
Newly arrived in these holy heights,
Having traveled from Mayan lands
To be joined together before the gods
At the very tip of the world.

—*David Bowles*

21

DOWNPOUR

Afternoons, with the punctuality
of tourist-filled regional jets,
cloud gathers, roils, darkens
and bursts into drenching rain
complete with fireworks show
and cranked-up Dolby sound.
Tourists scurry for shelter,
pack every *restaurante y cantina*
in the entire town. From stools
beneath a thatched canopy
we enjoy *tapas y cerveza*.
Below us, tiled roofs
spin rushing tinseled ropes,
deepen from muted terra-cotta
to glistening orange. My companion
mentions how *tapas* sounds
very similar to *topless*, offers
an exaggerated lascivious wink.
We stroll arm in arm
to our hotel as showers dwindle.
Droplets crown us with iridescence.

—*Ann Howells*

THE ELOPEMENT

I wanted to elope, almost fifty
years ago—I wanted the ladder and to drive
across into Mexico and Get Hitched
with two strangers to wish us well,

but instead there was the wedding mass,
thrown bouquet, everyone I ever knew
coming to the surface of the day and
sinking back into the crowd like goldfish.

I think sometimes about eloping
still, only with my last suitor,
the dark one. In the middle of a party
I've fled to my room, he opens the window

on the night stars and the great rush of air,
music and balloons and laughter
going on below us, nobody
even to know I've gone.

—Janet McCann

HUSBAND, IN MEXICO

I. *Piloncillo*
   Dark syrup
   one lick
   at a time

II. *Chocolate*
   Expected
   sweet
   feast

III. *Café*
   I brace
   myself
   for more

IV. *Corazón*
   Wilfull
   muscle
   afire

—*Sarah Cortez*

THE PARROTS OF PUERTO VALLARTA

Midnight. We chattering tourists, tamale
filled and Dos Equis soaked, wake the caged
birds who make drowsy attempts to answer,
tuck curved beaks under iridescent wings,
close their eyes, fall away into a lost sky.

In the morning, I call them *macaws*, the word
parrot too melodious for their shrieks and squawks,
jarring without a jungle chord beneath them.
I stand in a ring of droppings that paint
the concrete around their hotel cage
and apologize. I explain it is their beauty,
our lack of wings, makes us crazy to capture
and contain. Something in green feathers
we crave. Something in the flare of orange
above beaks that bewitches. They cock their
heads, listen eye to eye as if no one
had ever spoken gently to them before.

At the beach, teenagers parasail over
the Gulf, rise on fiesta-colored umbrellas
to claim the sky. These fledglings feel
the thrust of wind, see the planet's edge
curve, watch fish jump in the sun's glare.
They point their cameras at passing birds,
then on themselves soaring in blue space.
Laughing and screaming, they are winched
back to earth, bodies aflame with flight
that burned away their words, left them
squealing and screeching on the sand.

—*Carolyn Dahl*

AT EL MESÓN DE LOS POETAS

In this country the moon has risen closer to me.
It's still your moon, the one you tossed here
like a discus in the dark. This white seed that blooms
on my face like a kiss. I know you sent it. I know
your body lies down on rough sheets and when you close
your eyes you have already moved out of it—

opening into darkness—early sheep grazing the fields,
cacti and the curl of mesquite burning on the hillsides.
You visit me among thin crusts of custards,
the poinsettias and wrought iron benches,
in a wind that garnishes my hair with leaf tassels.
The waiter wants to usher me into the safety
of a wood paneled room but I would not see
the balconies and their bright striped umbrellas,

the old woman in an orange shawl and her basket
of fresh *bolillos*. There is no geography of blue—
no place to feel you beyond the closed doors
of your body.

—*Lois P. Jones*

PHOTOGRAPH OF AN INDIAN GIRL, CHIAPAS

Somewhere between seven and ten years old,
a Mayan girl of the Tzotzil or Tzeltal branch,
you inhabit this world like a grasshopper.
Nourish the maize-filled chamber of the heart:
its sere grasses, the latent, pounding rain.

Because I can already read your fortune
I am woven through with longing
split into strands brighter than the cloth in Zinacantán.
That village of flowers
shimmering like colored glass: mirage.

Because you will walk this dusty road
again and again with your mother, your friends,
the neighbors who shoot firecrackers at the moon,
your life and the lives of all who walk with you
will wear it down. Where else can you go?

If I could defy physics I would step
into this picture. Startle the photographer
who took it one morning when the ocelot yawned.

Pulling an orange ball from my pocket,
I would hurl it toward the clouds.

Watch you leap.

—Peter Ludwin

DIEGO ON MY MIND

Were he mine and I his,
        I would make it so
he could never escape
        from these tines
about my asking face.
        Forgive me.
I cannot hope to
        understand
this part of you that needs
        and needs
but does not desire
        that part of me
that drinks from your sweet soil.

        There were
darker dreams than you,
        and kinder
I have since known.
        I see them all.
Dreams of my death
        and dreams
by which to myself
        I am born.
Visions of staunch
        and of flow
and visions of a swollen tide
        to sweep away
this ever knowing you at all.

        And yet,
without your eclipse,
        I feel not
life,
nor death,
        nor barely living.
I crown me quiet like
        the Tehuanas
on the banks

of your exile,
but by your moon on my
     black lake,
you guide me back
     and I am home.

—Erin O'Luanaigh

HOMESICK

It's in the clay, you know—
the tropical memory of all things.
I try to avoid Mexican pottery for my flowers,
reaching only for Italian—
clay used to Italy's frigid seasons
settles in cozy up here.

The first Panhandle winter,
Mexican pots crack,
the homesick clay yearning for
poinsettias, bougainvillea,
tarragon, warm shovels,
the white heat of home.

I hear them crying at night
as they huddle in the first frost;
terra-cotta hearts broken by dawn.

—karla k. morton

PORTRAIT OF MEXICO

I enter the bramble of your hair, sketch
thorns in your ear, trace the line
of your chin. Its hammock curve holds
your face in its cusp. Hornets fill
your mouth: the buzz of lace,
a hive of vowels. Your iris smells
of cinnamon bark, your hair-bound
forest of coriander. Charcoal rivers unfetter
black swans nesting in your skull.
A bell rings in your nostril. The pigeons
are uprooted. Your collarbone
harbors the stain of mulberry. A thin
part through your hair separates east
from west. Above your brow an open
ocean. In your right eye, a half-moon,
in your left an eclipse. Your tongue
tangles with driftwood, thistle, ocotillo,
I want to taste the humming in your ear.

—Kate Kingston

MEXICO: ALWAYS GLISTENING

CAFÉ SAN MARTÍN

Do you remember the Café San Martín?
I do, sometimes,
when it rains in the afternoon and it's summer.
We liked to go there and drink coffee
and smoke while we looked at the rain.
The Café San Martín was small,
lukewarm, and it had big windows
that looked onto a meridian of June.
     But it is no longer there.
Now on that corner where it was
they sell video games.
Have you tried to go back?
Have you walked in the rain, alone,
remembering the girl you were
and asking yourself where would these people have gone,
with their pink curtains and old spoons
and their Café San Martín?
     Yes, I have wanted to go back,
many times,
when I happen to think of you,
when my shoes fill with water
and I wish I were that age again
and not so foolish
as to let go of your hand that afternoon.
     Once again it is June and raining.
Everywhere there are cafés
in certain neighborhoods.
     The present erases all traces.

—*Agustín Cadena*
translated by C.M. Mayo

TRIAGE

We ride in the *caisse* (wrong language)
of a big pickup truck with *los manos*
de compaña (right language),

a fence of scavenged lumber
to keep us in. They sit knees
folded and offer a spot

for me to stand. I'm here
for the ruins and the fish.
A ride *al mercado* for me,

bananas and gravel-scraping silence.

Then the old school bus to Mérida,
caged chickens on top. Another lift,
this time against a moped's bare muffler.

El tendero chips ice for my burn.
He hands it to me like a ticket.

I take it from him like a diamond.

—Martha Serpas

ON DAYS LIKE THIS, UNDONE

for my wife, 12.24.2013

On days like this with shopping left to do,
or tomorrow with meals to make
and mess to undo, or any of those that follow
with homework to strafe through and needs
piling up at your feet, days when we pass
in the hallway getting ready our separate lists,
or pass each other on the road carting kids
to practices on opposite sides of town,
this is the peace I wish for you—

Your toes spreading in the sand.
Your beach chair tilted into the sun.
I hear sunsets are lovely off Manzanillo
year around, so there and that, for sure,
with fish seared just right on both sides,
served with tortillas fresh from someone else's work.
So don't move, wife, the Pacific will whisper.
Slow your mind. Let the breeze stir
this sand, confectionary. The beer
is already within reach, almost
        too cold to drink.

—*Jack B. Bedell*

LAURELS FROM INDIA (OAXACA)

It's ten before noon. The bells ring
as if announcing the heat, the day
like a boy with his wooden fan
who whines from the shadows.

One woman chooses the brightness,
a chair in the sun, the sweat
pouring from her, the light on her back
and neck and hair,

while the bells, urgent, long, diachronic,
like the shallow, translucent edge of a river
at its uncut, eddying bank,
curl back upon themselves

in a swirl of self-return, their slow
persistent, offshore center
as deep and cool as a kind of winter—
all that water sounded against itself,

the part that it can carry, measured
in its depth, fish and mountain-
ice and shells and the bones
of small birds. At last, as a crowd gathers,

the heat assumes its familiar form,
accumulates into a fullness,
a perpetual hovering, like a dragonfly
tattooed on a white girl's upper arm,

an image of half-sleep and drowse,
the ancient epoch of a dream
drawn on the body. Soon,
a band starts up. Brass,

the cathedral behind it, musicians almost
leaning against the cool stone as they play,
the song like a small French circus
with a limber girl spinning in air.

They say they are going to cut
the laurels down, those gentle centuries,
there where Eisenstein and Lowry sat
in shadow, the green night at the height

of going. Each spring the jacaranda
bloom, a violet haze upon the land,
the framboyan like an orange
umbrella, the bright gown

of a sad virgin. But next year, too
soon, with its hermetic, umbilical knot,
you can't imagine it—undone—
the great trees uprooted.

—*Randall Watson*

MORELIA

Like a monarch butterfly, I float
over the plaza where the palms have
trunks painted white and I see my child
as she eats a brilliant mango on a stick.

Over the plaza where the palms have
waved at the Cathedral, I smile
as she eats a brilliant mango on a stick
in Morelia. This city of schools and songs

waved at the Cathedral, as I smile
seeing my child, a little *mariposa monarca*
in Morelia, this city of schools and songs.
I recall from a long lost time still here

seeing my child, a little *mariposa monarca*
dancing through the palm trees of Morelia.
I recall from a long lost time still here
floating towards some future in my mind,

dancing through the palm trees of Morelia,
visions of the dazzling aqueduct and the parks
floating towards some future in my mind
where children and butterflies,

visions of the dazzling aqueduct and the parks,
lead me far away in time yet bring me home
where children and butterflies sing
Morelia, this city of schools and songs.

—*Tony Mares*

THE INNOCENCE I BOUGHT AT THE BORDER

Her apron pockets are tightly packed
with red roses wrapped in newspaper pages
and tied with twine, for sale, except
she is only four and not sure
how to count the money.
I look into her deep brown eyes,
take a bundle of roses, smooth
the river in her hair. I cross
the Rio Grande back into Texas
with home-grown roses picked
from that little girl's heart.

—*Loueva Smith*

PYRAMIDS, MEXICO

for Ben and Hilary Barrera

A Spanish teacher and two students
in gray dusk and rain, we climbed
the Pyramid of the Sun, our feet
tentative on wet narrow steps.
Ben's voice, calm as the rain,
gave us history.
                   Two years later,
he died of cancer. His nameplate
lingered on his office door,
an artifact of a gentle life.

I loved the other student,
Hilary, his daughter. A dog
circled on top, wagged a greeting,
pushed his paws into my chest
till I led him down.

*

On top of the Pyramid of the Moon
the rain stopped. Behind haze
we saw the sun diffused. Down
the long road between pyramids
the dog ran.

I stood for a long time
in the silence of that small, flat space
with Hilary, Ben. We watched the dog
turn into a black spot.

I wanted to hug them then,
to press our wet skin together.
It was a little embarrassing,
all that love just welling up.
I just watched that spot disappear,
watched where the spot should be.

*

All deaths pile up inside one pyramid.
Ben's, one of my first. He was like that dog,
a black spot disappearing, gone.

If he were alive, he would still be
disappearing, and Hilary,
alive and disappearing from my memory.

I was nineteen—the wild roar
of love washed over me like the wind
on that great height.

Hilary and I practiced Spanish on the bus,
sweating our silhouettes against plastic seats.
Our shoulders touched. I stumbled over
simple greetings.

*

Dear Ben, dear Hilary,
I don't remember much else about that place—
was there an altar for human sacrifice?
Did I put my neck down on the slab?

I kept a diary in Spanish for the class.
I can barely read it now, black dogs,
black dogs running across the pages.

—Jim Daniels

WE ARE OF A TRIBE

We plant seeds in the ground
And dreams in the sky,

Hoping that, someday, the roots of one
Will meet the upstretched limbs of the other.

It has not happened yet. Still,
Together, we nod unafraid to strangers.

Inside us, we know something about each other:
We are all members of the secret tribe of eyes

Looking upward,
Even as we stand on uncertain ground.

Up there, the dream is indifferent to time,
Impervious to borders, to fences, to reservations.

This sky is our greater home.
It is the place and the feeling we have in common.

This place requires no passport.
The sky will not be fenced.

Traveler, look up. Stay awhile.
Know that you always have a home here.

—Alberto Ríos

NEAR MEXICO CITY

at the sounding
of the bells
before sundown,
ravens unravel

from the belfries
like black,
satin ribbons
loosed from the hair

of virgins.
The shadows,
laden with the scent
of incense and roses,

lengthen beneath
the gaze of peasants
suspended
in lavender air.

—*Larry D. Thomas*

1946: THE WAR IS OVER

I am eight. Military ships fill
San Diego Harbor. Spirits
are high; scarcity everywhere. I
sleep on a daybed in grandmother's
bedroom, my two aunts crammed
under the eaves of an attic dorm.

             Tijuana
is minutes away, a playground
for shopping filled with the brightest
colors. *Serapes*, painted pottery, paper
flowers spill onto sidewalks. Smells
fill the air: tacos, tamales, *pan dulce*
served on brown butcher paper,
the stink of a small donkey
where I sit for a souvenir photo.

My aunt buys me a hand-tooled
change purse smelling of cow. I
will carry it for years. The crowded
streets echo with laughter; guitar
notes mingle from bar to bar.
Walking becomes a dance. Barefoot
children run free in the streets, arches
flashing a paler music, footprints
left on dusty cobbled bricks. My feet,
strangled in laced-up Buster Browns.

Even the littlest girls have golden
studs in their ears. Earrings that I
am not allowed. Instead, I buy their
Chiclets. Two pieces of gum in a tiny
cardboard box and I wish, for a moment,
for something then unknown to me,
something hidden in the gaiety
of shopping with my aunts in a place
             called Mexico.

—Germaine Welch

XALAPA

For a month, now, I have been walking the city.
I like the way the girls rest their hands on their boyfriends'
    shoulders
to adjust a shoe.
The way a man bends over, back to the wind, to light a
    cigar.
How the gypsy women roam the park in their long dresses
    seeking donations.
Their faded brochures. The boys in fandango outside
    the cathedral.

And the smell of grease and oil at the little garage
is familiar and comforting. The chime of a ratchet or
    wrench
dropped in a toolbox. The graceful and threatening
loops of razor wire
coiling the wall-tops. Glass and mortar. Rebar
piercing the unfinished columns of houses.
Prayer flags of drying laundry. Lace and cotton.

Sometimes I walk long into what they say is a danger.
    The tin
communities. Doors slanting like a blade. Little braziers
glowing in the shallow interiors. Glassed candles
barring the windows. A lisping kettle.

But at my little house I can burn a fire too. I can hang
my jacket from the canisters of gas
that lean against the kitchen wall. Green steel.
The color of fine sand. Sunday's trumpeter
ascending the *calle*, waking the roosters.

Sometimes Maliyel, my landlady, invites me over
for camel straights and espresso. *Socorro*, she tells me,
is not some kind of wind, but one
of the names of sadness. Things
we are strong for. Assistance. Succor.
Then her son, Galo, calls down
from his sleeping loft, Randáll, *¡buenos días!*

Last night, at the *Téatro, Endgame.*
Capacity, eighty-five.
Maliyel said Beckett was like a cluster of pins
stuck in a wooden table
shining in a desk lamp's half-dollar
halogen brightness. All mauve at the margins,
like a nineteenth century curtain.
And she wondered if metaphor revealed a unity
hidden in the shape of things. What Paz conjectured.
How vision can resolve into a hardness. An encrusted
    geode.
Sun and stone. Speckles of quartz in the granite slab.

But this morning Galo and I play soccer.
I call it soccer because I live in Houston.
Maliyel comes out to watch, and is smiling.
He moves the ball between his feet, delicate,
precise, easing it with the outside of his foot
before he shoots. And we welcome it as it enters
into the air. There is nothing to protect. Nothing
to save. It is quite beautiful as it rises.

—*Randall Watson*

LOCALS LISTEN TO THE MARIACHI
BAND AT EL JARDÍN IN SAN MIGUEL

You see their silhouettes along the stone wall
or arm in arm below the glow of garden lights
huddled like foothills, earth you could plant maize in.

Cowboy hats and serapes, the smell of beer and
cinnamon churros. You think of *family* and *language*
how the music rolls through your hips

to the sweat behind your knees. How it rushes
through you, to a place you still don't know.

—*Lois P. Jones*

MOLE

Spicy sauce
flavored with chocolate
permeates the thighs, legs
and breasts of hens.
Its redolence,
seeping from ovens,

wafts through each
and every room
of the houses,
seeking sleeping newborns
to drift down to
like a blanket;

ease beneath their trembling
eyelids; and with its soft,
swirling brush,
color the irises
of the sparkling, little planets
of their eyes.

—Larry D. Thomas

TRANSFIGURATION

Convento y Iglesia de San Agustín, Salamanca, Mexico

I.
Entering under the plain streetside façade and looking up,
the fumes of the city's petroleum refineries lessening,
eyes adjusting to the dimness, one sees a new city,
this one of cherubim and seraphim. Apostles extend their
    hands,
bishops wield their mitres, Jesus and his mother ever
    suffer
amidst candles, crowns, leaves, and vines. The countless
    drapes,
sweet eyes, quiet wings, smooth feet are covered in pure
    gold.

II.
The Guanajuato Symphony sits ready behind the altar rail.
It is on state tour, with guest maestro, *el director huesped*
from *El Valle de Tejas.* Tonight they are playing Salamanca,
a post-Conquest city a-fume with oil refineries,
    industrialists,
cantinas, food vendors, and always the poor—booked
    into this
rare gathering place, a church begun in 1641 by
    Augustinians
and their *indio* converts, finally dedicated in 1706.

III.
Seven p.m. and by the guest conductor's compulsion to
    his gringo watch,
it is time to begin, the polished instruments hungry for
    their notes,
thousands of practice hours itching in the fingers and
    lips of the players.
For an audience, there are five scarved *viejitas*, come
    lately off the street,
old women possibly here only for warmth, for rest, for
    succor.

Signal given, the concertmaster appears from the
    transept, back straight,
refusing dismay at the empty seats, this latest affront
    to his art.

IV.

Equally stoic, the orchestra tunes and the maestro
    crosses from the sacristy,
his formal tails blacker than the robe of the priest who
    introduces him
and his musicians, says a prayer of consecration to the
    glittering walls.
The maestro taps his music stand with his baton,
    raises his arms,
and as the poster on the streetside plaster wall has
    announced,
"Oberatura de la Opera 'El Barbero de Sevilla'" fills the
    empty nave.

V.

Following the final chord there may come with luck that
    blessed second
of silence wherein a listener transitions back into the
    world. Tonight,
in that interval and in this place, the conductor dreads
    for his players,
for Rossini, for himself the hollow claps of five pairs of
    old hands.
But when he turns to face this meagerness, here's a
    tsunami of joy,
sanctuary roaring approval, bravos, feet stamping the
    cold Byzantine tiles.

VI.

The sound rises, keeps on rising into the golden filigree
    of the ceiling,
for while Rossini reigns, the church has filled with folk
    silent as mice at midnight,
bowing to the niches, crossing themselves, sliding into
    the pews,
filling row on row in their own good time, come, after all,

to hear their symphony orchestra, to banish with
 strings and trumpets
and flutes and tympani the great hungers of their
 hearts.
They are bartenders, demimondes, architects, nursing
 babes
mujeres elegantes, doctors, street vendors, barefoot
 children,
teens come lately in uniform from school, architects,
 nuns.

VII.
The *director huesped* wonders if they should start the
 concert over,
considering who has heard what, but now he presses on
with the program: Schubert's Unfinished Symphony,
 an obce fantasia,
the finale as Ippolitov's "Escenas Caucasianas," each
 time
the people on their feet, with long clamorous applause
 and shouting.
This night is filled with the joy of the wide world—music
 of Italy Austria,
Los Estados Unidos, Russia, played by Mexicans for
 their countryfolk
both *pobres* and world-renowned oil advisors of
 Salamanca, here
in the cocoon of Mexican Churrigueresque architecture
built by the Spanish Augustinians and their mestizos,
 here
in this nest of universe speaking in concert *en verdad*
the language of music through centuries and cultures,
all the while, golden saints and angels listening from
 above.

—*Jan Seale*

ON THE HIGHWAY OF THE SUN

four lanes through the pink mountains
link Acapulco to Mexico City

the most beautiful 165 miles
in Mexico's financial death march

a privatized artery no longer feeding the heart
of machete-wielding peasants
eager to slash coconuts for thirsty travelers

and kids wearing worn-out iguanas
cheap at twice the price

it runs past the Tequesquitengo sugar mill
Cortes built on cane slavery

and the pit where fighting roosters
swear and spit behind the spa's walls
then on beyond Cuernavaca

where Lowry's Consul tried to drink
himself to death in a foothills cantina

and villages where the bedbug hauler
sits throttling his engine

and exhausted men collect
around picnic tables
as evaporative coolers

blow aside dreams as easily
as the smell of grilled chicken

but if you saw this Mexico
you would understand

why donkey-eared Lampwicks
like us drive on
still yearning for Pleasure Island

and dreaming of Coronado's gold
always glistening just beyond
the horizon where all roads end

—*Jerry Bradley*

MEXICO: PRAYER BLOSSOMING A PATH

SUMMONS

The spry hustle
of a young coyote
holds a mourning dove
limp in its jowl. He trots
past the roadside shrine
of broken glass, river rocks
and *milagros* made of silver.
There are rosary beads and
a holy card of Our Lady
of Guadalupe. Her palms
turned open, tacked
in a handmade box.

—*Kathleen Markowitz*

A PLACE TO WAIT

Under the cathedral's white stone towers
is not a place for a Protestant
to come alone on Good Friday.
Christ is almost naked inside.
Crystal-throated boys sing
extravagant refrains. Soprano
hymns pour thousands of wings
revolving in unison out through the wide doors.
Whatever is being said are not words
but whole families. I don't know
a prayer as insatiable
as the resurrection.
This is not a place for a Protestant
to have her feet washed. Ritual
songs as persistent as roots
twist around the wrists of ankles
of all of us waiting to enter and bow down
within the cool darkness shimmering
in candle-flame prayers
as turbulent as a night ocean swelling.

—*Loueva Smith*

BORDER TOWN

A skeleton pulls a chair to the bar,
red eyes glittering rubies. He prattles on
about the *Ladinos*. The ladies

who work on his petite theaters.
All day they paint the dead
in miniature. Cutouts of Kahlo's head

float on strips of wood.
He knows all the rituals,
Santa Elena de la Cruz

who takes nails from the Cross
pinning her lover's heart
to make him loyal.

Twelve hours later I'm still
on this damn bus to Zacatecas.
A hell ride south through candlewood

and trash. The bus slows down
for construction, just enough time
to see a man emerge from the market.

He looks directly at me, eyes pitted
from too many Coronas. I think of Jesus
and how he called my cell but never left

a message. Hung himself above my bed
at Posada de Las Monjas in room 26.
His breath seeping from rusted pipes

above the fireplace. *Listen, Jesus, Santa Elena*
has taken a nail from your cross and used it
to pin her lovers. Tell me,

Why do they leave? The bus picks up again.
Jesus joins the burros up ahead
and never looks back.

—*Lois P. Jones*

MEXICO CITY: 36 HOURS

Each jolt surely the end, the bus gasps
at last alongside a two-hundred-year-old church
whose hungry faithful—thousands of them—flock
beneath rigged speakers. It's Easter.

For a peso we queue up to lunge past
glinting inlay. The conveyor belt lurches
as we look up to Ascending Jesus. Neon
halo winking as his hands weep.

—*Margo Davis*

FIRST TASTE

We only knew Mexico as a carnival—
a taste of exotic one week at a time;
spirals and dazzling lights and mariachi music—
an irresistible piper a few blocks from home.

She'd appear overnight—all oranges and reds;
paper flowers in her hair—
and we, young and hungry,
craving everything about her—

her fluttering language,
swift as birds;
our heads cocked like hounds
for breadcrumbs of English.

But one night, my brother and I ventured alone;
stuck upside-down on the Hammer ride,
the shoddy lap bar
squealing loose from the weight of us;
bolts quivering;

my new confirmation necklace
hanging over my head,
destined for the asphalt one story below;

my brother braving one hand to catch it;
Jesus' silver face
clutched in his fist.

And when we were finally let down,
dizzy from the blood in our heads
and eyes and ears,
we held on to each other,
glimpsing the driver's own
silver savior—
a pistol wedged tight in his jeans;

the language curdling dark and metallic;
pricking the hair on our necks—
the first time we ever tasted
the black current of violence;

Jesus clasped tight between our palms
as we ran.

—karla k. morton

THE BORDER BLASTER

On my father's route from Uvalde to Alpine
I was lying flat on the back seat of his 1958 Ford Fairlane.
Jesus promised to save me in a language I couldn't
    understand.

My father would turn the radio way down at night so I
    could sleep
but he would lay the top of the car down so I could look out.
On some nights, like tonight, it seemed as if
the stars were shrugging and shedding their patina of dust;

the sky was milky with blessing, spread out and glistening.
I remember my father would say, "Only English when
    we get there.
You have been here before. You know how to act."
I knew when we finally stopped in the morning
the teeth of his comb would catch in my wind-tangled hair.

We would drive through the night sometimes, like tonight,
the dot on the radio dial a little beacon.
There was only one station on the radio,
Jesus shouting he would save us, in Spanish, only
    Spanish.
We had a trunk full of shoes and boots and belts
and brochures, lots of brochures, all of them in English.

At night, driving, my father's brown hands would turn
    black,
He was a shadow at the wheel. I was a smaller shadow
    in the back.
I sat up in the seat, let the wind blow the Mexican words
    out of my head
so I would know what to say when I got to Alpine.

Pelo. Tonight I would let that word go, let it tangle
in the mesquite our car was rushing by. I decided tomorrow
I would lose *baile.* I closed my eyes, sorting words like
    star dust,
while Jesus promised to bless us in a language I couldn't
    understand.

—*Alan Birkelbach*

ALL NIGHT BUS

With a push and shove
I board the dirty, dented bus.
It lurches forward, jerks
the roof riders clutching
racks and bleating goats.

In a seat for two, three of us squeeze. Sandwiched
in the middle, I press against the aisle sitter's
body, half of which balances on a sliver of seat, the other
half suspends over the air of the aisle, held in place
by the push of another body from across the gap.
Caught in a bridge, the two men levitate like magicians
over the abyss, conjuring seats where none exist.

Daylight disappears into smudges, flares briefly
in fractured window cracks, confusing the rooster
who crows beneath a man's serape. Sometimes
we skid to a stop in the desert's nowhere, drop
a family into shadows, their goat leading
the way home through starlight and scorpions.

Shouldn't I be afraid? Saguaros rise from the dark,
thick arms raised like bandits who might be real.
I am a woman alone, know no Spanish, riding with
strangers and a driver who is high on peyote,
in a rickety bus leaking carbon monoxide. Yet,
what I feel is peace. I trust the dusty Madonna
pasted to the bus wall, her hand raised in perpetual
blessing. I find comfort in fussing babies under
mothers' rebozos, smelling tortillas, the soft breaths
of the aisle sitter whose head has nodded onto my shoulder.

I have the luxury of choice. Yet, I chose this box of souls
rattling over rock-studded roads on patched tires and
rusted axles. I don't sleep but watch the driver's rosary
    swing
from the mirror. I hold my place in this moment like
the aisle sitters hold each other over the abyss till morning.

—Carolyn Dahl

ON NARROW STREETS

In San Miguel, the Blessed Virgin
    Mary still walks. I've seen her
        inside a window, opulent gold dress

billowing against scorching truck headlights.
    Her Baby's stiff, dark cowlick;
        her own glistening, smudged blue

eye shadow. At the market, the smoke
    of outdoor sizzling meats rises
        to her serene face by the fruit

and vegetable stalls. Her portico wall
    pocked with full niches of dazzling
        red and white roses, bundled.

Her own small fingers, a reverent
    brown tent above haggling flies
        and loud commercial buzz.

Only in the great church are she
    and her Baby rosy. His dimpled chest
        above a grey blanket, one hand lifted

in an infant's calm salute to the safe
    unknown. Heavenly Mother and Son here
        proffer a pearl rosary. Iridescent

bulbs of hope. Lustrous lozenges
    of fervid prayer blossoming a path
        out of our own particular dark.

—Sarah Cortez

DAY OF THE DEAD

Today, the air
of Mexico everywhere
is clamoring
with the jangling
of the bones.

Clad in the costumes
of skeletons, the children
drag their shuddering tongues
across the crowns
of candy human skulls

under festive skeletons
of all sorts and sizes
dancing in the sky,
grinning, their eye sockets
stuffed with blood-red roses.

Even the gravestones
are granted a brief reprieve
from the cold,
turned by widows
into tables of warm food,

widows busily engaged
in dimpling their fingertips
with the magical,
faceted beads
of black rosaries.

—*Larry D. Thomas*

DE UN DÍA, OF A DAY

The one-eyed dog of Rufino Tamayo
Awakens the sun and drags it over the hill
By the hem of its blazing raiment,
Startling the spirits who cease their night mischief.
Rattling fetishes, they retreat over the cobblestones,
Hounded by the day, chased by church bells.
Desiccated leaves clatter up the hill
With the wind like the sound of feet without flesh,
Without shoes, the scrabbling
Of frightened bones in motion.

From behind wooden doors
Shut like coffins against the night,
Still sleeping women with terra cotta faces
Rise in their dreams to sweep away
What night has left in its wake.
Slishing fistfuls of water from leathery hands
Onto the dawn cooled floor,
They calm the feathery dust and banish
The devil's dandruff into the street
With brooms of twig.

Feathers, flowers, eggs and apples,
Photographs of those who sleep in the dust
Adorn the shrine of the weeping virgin
At the roadside where men in suits of white cotton stop
As day expels night from along the far horizon
Like an explosion of mirrors.

This day the dog has brought is stout with the muscle of
        the sun.
Wavering apparitions, women bringing lunch to men in
        the fields
Float over the shimmering earth, suspended in the heat
Like birds wheeling in the blind sky.

Beyond the rim of the day, the one-eyed dog
Circles a spot and tamps for himself

A bed in the tall grass
While around the plaza, the evening processional begins
As minstrel skeletons play their instruments
From the filigreed bandbox
For the dancers waltzing in earth-eaten finery.

—*AM Krohn*

MILAGROS

Here is a small silver hand, only one
so you may not hear it clapping
nor see it grasp the faint possibility of healing
in the incense-rich air of the chapel.

A pair of brass mountains represent sensation
and responsiveness to touch. They pray away
the cancer cells that prey on one lumpy breast
and threaten to infiltrate a woman's countryside.

This tiny foot kicks upward toward angelic choirs
when they sing but fail to intercede for the lame.
This rooster crows awake *santos* slow
to make things happen in the barnyard.

Here is a suspended arm that knows the time
it takes to heal a break and the way
a lover's separation makes life seem
like one lone arm embracing mist.

These base-metal molded talismans
are men and women on their knees.
At night, when candle light is snuffed
and potent waters trouble the font, they inch
their supplicant way past side chapels to kneel
before the tabernacle of their transubstantiated Lord.

The head of a woman in silhouette represents
her loftiest thoughts, mostly directed to God,
but a passing few shot toward the crotch
of the man who offered the *milagro*
and prays daily for her prurient goodness.

A *milagro* of a peaked-roof house was pinned
to the skirt of the church's dark Virgin
in hopes of calling forth a home. The family's former hut
is buried under treeless mud that came sliding
off the hillside in last season's unrelenting rains.

A gold-tone sleeping infant might mean the Jesus child
or perhaps the sickly *niño* at home in the suspended
     wooden bed
or the born-dead baby who talks to his mother in her sleep
asking nightly for another chance.

That exquisite silver bird was not crafted as a *milagro* at all.
In its life as a scarlet tanager it nested on the sill beneath
wrought-iron grillwork over Hermalinda's window.
When Romero commissioned the *bruja* to make Hermalinda
     love him,
the bird flew into her chapel, constricting into precious
     metal
and silencing bird-song along its final flight.

A ex-voto in the shape of a donkey hangs on the robe of
     St. Francis.
It has served to heal the lame ass that serves the Valdez
     family—
all of whom glance its way as they walk past after
     communion.

Hungry Paulito bought one pig *milagro* with his last few
     pesos
when he had a powerful craving for bacon.
He traded his coins for a pig-shaped investment
in the hope of a someday full stomach.

This selfless offering of a pure gold heart with corona
     of barbs
sends healing balm and redress
to each slighted lover, abandoned mother, crying child,
every heart pierced through with a dagger of indifference
every wounded soul of deflated expectation
every newborn left nursing its own lower lip.

—Maureen Tolman Flannery

WANTING DAWN

The chachalacas fuss about the growing night,
cacophonies of love complaining with contrite
yet angry hearts that roosting in mesquite belies
their hunger for abundance and collective rise.

—*Patrick Allen Wright*

MEXICO: LABYRINTH OF LABYRINTHS

SMALL FIRES

my grandfather's house at the edge of a landfill
the turn from the highway to the dirt road
my grandfather standing with his hat in his hands
the mesquite trees' broken twigs feeding small fires
my mother bought him a TV a truck helped him build a
    fence
my grandfather's house of rats ruminating in the sun
the lines of traffic cars split off my mother's knuckles
    white
the stories of the conquistadores end like this
my grandfather's gold tooth showing when he smiled
my mouth dry for hours on the road
the canals dividing the neighborhood the stories of
    the dead
my grandfather's house of grackles brushstrokes leaving
    a painting
the train tracks we knelt between to play games
the cracked egg in another boy's hand the beginning of a
    beak of an eye opening
the living in unfinished houses callused feet cinderblock
    coarse
my grandfather's hair slicked in waves of ash
the stories of the Aztecs end like this
newspapers where dead children keep appearing on the
    front page
my grandfather's house of cardboard and wood scraps
    his hat in his hands
a labyrinth of garbage a labyrinth of faces a labyrinth of
    labyrinths
they looked asleep in the backseat they would find their
stomachs cut filled with drugs
the stories of a new world end like this
my grandfather's house of flies thick words stumbling
    from the page
the mesquite the sap darker I had hours to look at it
my grandfather's house in the rain I asked got slapped
    for it would it sink or sail away

the stories I have to tell my mouth the road his hat in
    his hands
not a new world a world made new from what was here
my grandfather's prayers to a ceiling with holes in it
trains on the tracks only at night only in dreams
my grandfather's house of rain when he died the rain
    died too

—José Angel Araguz

LEARNING CURVE

Smoke that whispers among Tarahumara
ranchos says nothing about electricity
that will soon arrive, *telenovelas*

the women long to watch.
It speaks only the language of drought,
the curses of boys who don't want

to farm anymore because in Chihuahua,
they've heard, Cortés has landed again.
Inhaling this message,

I skirt Indian women washing laundry
in a creek, the vibrant colors
a suite of blossoms after cloudburst.

Farther on, a grizzled *viejo*
trails two burros loaded down with wood.
Now I drift deeper into Old Mexico,

cradle of myth, catch-basin of desire.
Seek the bones of Quetzalcoatl
as I devour silence like bread

dipped in wine's salty blood. By nightfall,
when the moon rises over Norogachi,
pale blue horses descend the arroyo.

Stringing translucent violins, they perform
sonatas for people moving to where horses
play no music. *In America*, their cousins

tell them, *horses make six figures.*
More cunning than when he married
ruse to Toledo steel,

Cortés brings the promise of boom boxes.
Of fast cars that need never know
the sierra's pot-holed ruts.

—*Peter Ludwin*

MEXICO

It will be the last time the U.S. Cavalry
will use horses in combat. Spads, Fokkers,
machine guns, tanks: all will see to that.
My grandfather is nineteen and hails from
Paterson, the filthy Passaic the river
he knows best. Now it's the Rio Grande
that greets him and his Army issue horse
whose name is Red. That much I know.
Harry. Harry Szymborski or Sembeski
or Sembooki, or however the census takers
spelled his name, what the hell difference
did it make? His parents worked the mills
along the Falls as weavers and machinists,
grinding work, and why he joined the Army.
Five eight, brown eyes, brown hair, bantam
weight, so the records say. In the photo
I have of him he's excised his face
so the eye can focus on his horse.

It's April, 1916, and he's part of the Expedition
going after Villa. He's saddled up and his carbine
glints, and soon he will be heading south
from Texas into Mexico after a shadow
the Army will never capture. Through endless arid
days and deserts, past blossoming cacti
and blue fevered skies and serpentine arroyos,
past the chalk-dry bones of men and cattle
flowing ghostlike backward by him,
he floats as in a dream, the language strange
and those who live there stranger, one
more U.S. soldier awakening to another
twilight nightmare: Okinawa, the Chosin
Reservoir, Khe San and Kuwait's smoldering
oil fields, then Kabul, until at last one arrives
in the Land of JubJub, one more Polish kid
following orders, one more benighted knight
sent out to make the world safe, at least for oil,
trudging back to Texas, then on to France,

where mustard gas will get him, having done
his part to end the war to end all wars until
the next one calls, and then the next, and
the twilit borders bleed together, as he goes on
doing what he must, until at last the very land
he rides upon along with Red his horse will have
long since turned to dust along with him.

—*Paul Mariani*

SACRED SAILORS OF THE GULF

Come lie with me,
you tired, broken sailors,
on the coast we've learned
so well. Turn up your palms
and palpate my grimy platypus skin.

Dance in the naked embrace
of the cratered moon
with the trampled grass
stabbing your back
like a comrade you'll never forgive.

Dream, sacred seamen,
of days when you lost
calloused fingers to the salted stones
of the shore when you were only trying
to lose your consciences.

Get down on your knees
on the graveled sand,
and admonish yourselves for dreaming
that I'd bless anything.

The smile of your toothless son?
The vivid swell of your dreams?

I am your pillaged illustration
of Mexican beauty, of your predilections
and the twisted realities of luscious mermaids
who listened to your thoughts
when your stubby wife had heard enough.

Please touch the left side of my chest
that's caving in
because I need a heart to hold
the sacrileged skin.

Blame everyone, but the sea
because when you drown
in water-wrought sorrow
you meet me.

—Elizabeth Humber

EATING CHIMICHANGAS IN ZACATECAS

Staring a baroque Cathedral framing
the Sierra Madre Oriental, electric signs
flashing Pancho Villa line the square ticking
to the 100ᵗʰ anniversary of his liberation

of Zacatecas. I fork the chimichanga
and laugh—the kitsch tease for foreign
tourists. Tex-Mex in the old capital
of the Mexico Norte selling itself

as local fare. The Greek diner
we are eating at sells no Greek
food, and barely any Norteño:
sketches by Dali and Rivera

line the diner like a coffee
shop wall, the prints subbing
for stucco. Funny how one
sells the idea of oneself back:

mezcal and chocolate, abandoned
nunneries, silver mines, central
mountain's wineskin curve, statues
to John Paul II. Beyond the colonial

streets, a few women dressed in
loose cotton blouses beg—sun-dried,
I drop her ten pesos in the cup.
What is stripped, left behind, rebuild

another bullshit search for authenticity
among quartz rosaries once mined
by thin-muscled Zacatecos until
their bellies burst in rock-heat.

None of this true alone. The border,
beyond which chimichangas birthed

in grease, was porous as the war
sliding it south. Villa died eight years

after the victory in the square, bullets
riddling his brain. His death mask hid
in Texas for nearly half-a-century, given
back like a faux native bead work jaguar:

toothless sentiment of the plastic dead.

—*C. Derick Varn*

MERCADO SAN JUAN

Such real and unreal colors and displays,
strange vegetables and fish, butchered beasts,
crisp loaves, flowers shiny-damp,
smell of garlic, spices, leather handbags,
shafts of sunlight falling between stands,
stall-keepers sharing in-jokes and embraces,

and the shoppers, mostly women, carrying
string bags or canvas, paper-wrapped parcels,
to take home lunch, soaps, souvenirs,
bright scarves, cheeses, skulls in sombreros,
sandals, watches, stopping to chat with neighbors
to be offered a taste of something salty,

something sweet. Seedlings in cups,
mushrooms frying in a skillet, ¡Mira!
toss the cucumbers in a bag, weigh it—
so we who have no community can pretend,
can borrow this one, leave hours later
heavier and lighter.

—*Janet McCann*

ISLA DE LA PIEDRA

The old man sleeps face down in the sand.
He dreams of pelicans squabbling over entrails

at Playa Norte, of gringos lined up
to ride his forlorn horses.

Once, I followed him through coconut
groves bordering the beach. His worn teeth,

a canvas of the *real* Mexico, grinned
their stained accounts of dung.

We grazed the surf,
and all I'd come for opened

like a field of lilies: sun, sea, sand
and sky bound together

like a shawl a *curandera* weaves
when the moon breaks its water.

You sit a horse well, Martín told me.
I assured him it was illusion,

nothing more, that my ease stemmed
from the John Wayne movies I'd seen.

But that was just the half of it.
Truth is, we were enacting

a prescribed role: a poet and a *viejo*
on two dumb beasts

living somewhere outside the body,
beyond the rigid boundaries of time.

—*Peter Ludwin*

BUS TOUR

in the museum. on the whirlplume.
the walls their lives. cleaning the bird.
eyes impassive, her hands making bread.

plumage whirling down the pole. bright air.
closer to earth and closer. round calendar.
concerned museum guide, you can not do that.

the ruins of ruins on the road
that leads toward Chiapas. broken wall.
clear cool day, so many people,

transactions. I buy, fill my arms
for the contact with theirs, the counting.
why am I here? the sky an even blue,

painted. weather of heaven. worn carved-face woman
I hand you, out of what? coins, gold-rimmed
unreal. cold in the palm. nothing.

gracias Señora. why am I here?
time wiped out, Aztec eyes,
Carlota, and the conquistadores

on the canvas together. the boundaries,
lines erased. a terrible beauty.
the blue of it. the implacable weather.

—Janet McCann

THE BURRO AND THE MAGUEY

Near the Pyramid of the Sun,
the Mexican guide stopped the car
to buy another six-pack of Carta Blanca.
He walked the visitors to a burro
tethered to a post beside a maguey,

popped the cap off a bottled beer,
stuck its neck into the burro's mouth,
slapped his thigh and guffawed
as the burro threw its head back,
guzzling the beer to the last drop.

He said, there in the old country,
even the burros craved *cerveza fria*.
Then, in a gesture of reverence,
he snapped the long, black thorn
a fleshy leaf of the maguey tapered to,

and pulled the long fibers attached to its end.
He held it proudly in the bright, Mexican sun,
touting it as a ready-made needle and thread
to the ancients; and to the moderns:
its fermented juice perfect for *pulque*, tequila.

—*Larry D. Thomas*

FRIDA

(Magdalena Carmen Frida Kahlo y Calderon)

There is no Mexico without Frida—
tiers of brilliant skirts
and braided hair,
shawls cast once, twice
about the shoulders.

She changed her birthday by three years
to match Mexico's Independence—
so they'd forever be linked in history
like lovers,
like crazy, passionate,
black-browed lovers.

We feel the self portraits
of a tortured life;
the betrayal of fate;
thorns of war around the throat.

But there's a picture of her—
blouse open to the waist,
two hands tight around a revolver.

Maybe this is the *real* Mexico—
the one so few get to see—

una casa azul that your father built;
the soft scent of frijoles on the stove;
a willing woman waiting;

knowing how easy it is to die;
the stiff grief of the living;
the garrison
of a little blue house;
a warm belly full of beans.

—*karla k. morton*

THE LADY BULLFIGHTER, PAT MCCORMICK

1953

The tiny bullring in Villa Acuña was a teacup
filled with ochred dust, odors of animals,
sweat and beer, rumbling voices, olés,
the pulsing heartbeat of a throbbing crowd.

Seats: sunny-side $2.00, shady-side $3.00.
Cerveza ads painted on the walls, faded words,
amputated letters here and there, the bulls, gladiators
     to entertain,
butted and banged against wooden walls down below.
The *restaurante* close by awaited *carne* for dinner.

She strutted like the best matador, a *torera*,
a woman invading machismo, *no traje de luces*
for her, she fought on foot, *a pie*, the red cape her wings,
dancing on her shoulders, she flew through the air.

No bouquets in a vase, but petal-showers over her dark,
bowed head, *estoque* in hand, the ears of the bull her gift
for bravery, for dancing in 300 *corridas*, enduring
beyond six gorings, outlasting the last rites, only her
sword and cape and heart in the yellow bright air.

—Sherry Craven

HOTEL JACARANDAS, 1972

The sand burns like a rumor that could ruin
you, although you don't know what this feels like
yet; a blinding white arena sears
your soles in Mazatlán. You're five years old.

Your grandma brought her maid, your pregnant mom,
your brother, you to Hotel Jacarandas. Dad
has stayed home. It's painful here.
Your scalding feet. People

staring—*¡Que linda güerita!* Firey
hair, chalky skin, blue eyes. Near
dinner time your mom zips
you into a white tulle dress and pulls

your hair so hard it hurts. You yelp; she yanks
grosgrain ribbons into bows and braids.
The restaurant is a round terrarium
of green fronds. Your mother worries

you, a loneliness inside.
An elderly, white-haired American
swings from his chair and *psssts* at you.
You jump and suck in breath.

Hello there, beautiful.

He's just attempting to be nice, your mom
says later, noticing you have not touched
your steak and baked potato. She drinks gin
with dinner; Grandma slurps her Blood and Sand.

The elderly American stops by
the table on his way back to his room.
You're sure that you don't want to marry me?
he says. You cringe. Your mother's eyes revive.

Oh, honey, slurs your grandma, *leave the child
alone*. Your mom grins at the gentleman
then asks Grandma to take you and your brother
to the room. You shake your head. You'll stay

here. Now. You can't leave her alone with him.
Your brother, Marco, starts to cry. *Okay,
okay, it's time to go*, your mother sighs.
She signs the bill, then heaves her body up

out of her chair, into the air, which starts
to strangle you. The gentleman grabs hold
of your mom's elbow, puts his other arm
around her waist helping her find her legs.

Outside, you keep your eyes trained on the ground,
alert for giant roaches. Never have
you seen such insects. They scare
you as much as this man: what can you do?

Your mom and the American man pause
along the pathway, whispering about . . .
you'd die to know. Her belly seems to float
in space relieved from *corpus mundi*, lovely

sacrament, the host that saves the world.
Where *is* your father? Why is he not *here*?
You press yourself against your mother's legs.
She pulls you closer, cups your ear within

her palm. Vibrations hum from underneath
her skin, confusing messages you wish
you could decipher: meaning craving making.
Your mother won't stop talking to this man.

You really want to get back to the room
where Grandma, Marco, and your grandma's maid
are probably watching television now—
noticias, concursos, anything

but what you're witnessing—because you can't
stand seeing your mom gleam beneath this moon,
her body bigger than your biggest fear,
which is that you will lose her, now and here.

—*Christa Forster*

MEXICO: A BROKEN PLACE

RECOVERING THE WOUNDED DEER

after frida kahlo

at once the deer wakes
    we step between broken
branches as the earth moves
    we walk but never closer never further
like tantalus' mouth to the dark lake
    the distance between us remains
we release arrows that reach her
    center her liver a trickle of dark
red and then a human ear appears
    below her doe ear

an arrow to her chest
    her face becomes cream smooth
another arrow and another until
    nine-filled she turns
her woman face to us
    it is our wives' faces
when she opens her mouth
    it is our wives' mouths
when she speaks it is
    our wives' voices   she says
they told me you would do this

now when we make love to our wives
    we cannot feel their warmth
though we burrow and hide
    in our dreams she returns
to us naked and full woman
    we say *we did not know we only tried*
we were so young but she tells us
    to close our eyes and we close them
she says *listen to me* and we listen
    she whispers
you will never be forgiven and we awake
    our hands curled and ready

—*Rebecca Young Eun Yook*

MERCADO DE HIERBAS

The market heat bakes in stale day
in the tostadas. We take our mid-afternoon
break during the siesta near the *tienda de
hierbas espirituales* in the center of bazaar:

candles for Santa Muerte, skeletal
and smiling in her evening
finery, candles for Pancho Villa to
pray for all the North so far from God,

so close to Texas, and row on row
of sage hung like nooses to cleanse
all the mold of human dry-rot away
from the cinder blocks and high walls.

We have been lucky, taxi drivers speak
slow Spanish or slower English, no shootings
for three weeks, no dead narcos or *federales*
near the Christo over the city. Saint Death

made a deal with Mictlantecuhtli, the candles
must be working. A woman offers me ceviche
from a kiosk beside, her hands leathered and
skin draped on her fame. I eat the fish slowly

noticing each piece cooked in acid, noting
the remnants of bone, even in peace, we
pray to her hand holding a globe and to
his toothed smile, once draped in owl feathers

and Aztec papers, now decorated in dollars
and rolling papers. So much sage, so much
dry laugher. I spit out the small bones left
from careless consumption, left for her.

—*C. Derick Varn*

PLAZA DE LA CONSTITUCIÓN

The view from Majestic's roof terrace stuns:
the Zócalo, the Governor's Palace to the east,
the altar of the kings in the cathedral,
the mint, museums, the academy of art.

The constitution was Spain's, not Mexico's,
but every September *El Presidente* recites the Grito
and pronounces Mexico free again.

It is where Axayácatl and Moctezuma's uncle reigned
and Cortes' palace was built on the bones of Aztec dancers
so every equinox viceroys could be sworn in
despite despots, earthquakes, and floods.

The Olympic marathon began here in '68,
and 18,000 bared themselves for a camera
near La Santisima, the church of the most holy
    sacrament,

and during Holy Week from a restaurant
in the Portal de Mercaderes we saw
striking teachers beaten with metal pipes.

—*Jerry Bradley*

WHAT HE LEFT BEHIND

topes lining streets
giggles walking hand in hand
braille beneath their feet

broom rustles up dust
kettle cries alongside the baby
her home, tilted hips

"Gone to USA"
stitched on her apron belly
his photo face down

—*Celeste Guzmán Mendoza*

NAVIGATING MEXICO

We drive through village
After thirsty village,
Down dusty streets
With walls on either side,
Miles of walls, adobe or cinderblock
Blank as a closed eye.

Some have glass or razor wire
On top. A few are staked
With palisades, iron spikes
Pointing up, hours of walls
Broken now and then
By gates with heavy hinges.

In Chiapas, one boy
Fires an imaginary gun
At us. A woman in Oaxaca
Looks up from her murky wash
To scowl.
One man throws a rock.

Walled off
Almost from each other,
We reach our hotel
At dusk. One gate opens
And the world
Dazzles into green.

Ferns hang in swaying baskets,
Fronds drooping like skirts
Of resting dancers.
Bougainvilleas and lemon trees
Spiral up toward night,
Their leaves fat like jovial tycoons.

And in the center
Of the fragrant dark
A fountain purls and shimmers,

Iridescent droplets everywhere
Cooling our sunburned faces
And boiling blood
Like a mother's calm embrace.

—*Carol Coffee Reposa*

INNOCENCE

There were no guns on the beaches of Acapulco,
only sand and sea and dots of boats here and there,
like floating balloons.

Xylophones danced their notes in salty air
at the club de la Rana perched like a frog
on the edge of a hill, cutting into the curve
of the road, a flag in the wind. Roqueta Island

across the bay, 30 miles out. Rumbas and cha-chas
stirred and shook the margaritas. We walked
streets with no thoughts but to buy blouses
embroidered with "Mexico" in crayon colors,

scurry through markets gorged with handmade
serapes, *platos y comidas deliciosas.*

Reminding us of Virginia's in Juárez, the indoor fountain
sang as we ate and then ambled along musky night-streets.

Danger and fear, greed and violence, never our
      companions
in the country of flowers and small back streets and
      gilded church
altars crimson roofs and holy bells tolling the minutes,
the everlasting minutes that are now not ours

but belong to money—the longing for—not for a lover,
but a bedfellow of dollars and dollars. The old story
—selling the soul–so then, who owns Mexico today?

—*Sherry Craven*

A BROKEN PLACE

The neighborhood where we once were,
we've heard, has long since disappeared:
bankruptcies filed and walk-aways,
though some transfers were neatly done.

We'd both been told before we went
the trash pick-up occurred three times
a week. That sounded civilized.
But garbage piles when we arrived
were stacked head-high and festering.
The city's new regime had just
found out that all the garbage trucks
had been sold off, but no one seemed
to know the enterprising thieves.
And other things came into view:
a fireball rolling up my arm,
and water boiling in the pipes,
a water heater whose fireball
burned my eyebrows off and scorched
my arms and face, and when I think
of that outrageous day, I think
of that damn worthless crew who told
me nothing there was wrong, that I
should just accept the limits of
machinery—it all breaks down.
A part of me, of course, agreed
with that. Another part said hell
with that—I'll not give up my life
or skin for this damn pissant place.

We're in, I told my wife, we're in,
I said, one sleepless night, a place
that does not work. She laughed and that,
of course, made sense, and I laughed too,
but not enough to change my mind.
The place would not begin to work
until the good ones here who said
competence and justice should

become a basic part of life
quit finding their tires and brakes
had been adjusted or—let's say
it straight—been tampered with or cut.
That happened to the man who lived
across the street. He'd been brought in
to sweep corruption out. And he,
his wife and sons were our good friends.
A careful man, his car sailed off
the road one day and onto jagged rocks.

—*James Hoggard*

ZARAGOZA PLAZA 6:00 A.M.

Smells of diesel fuel travel from the International Bridge
as passenger cars and commercial trucks travel between
    dos Laredos.

Outside La Posada hotel, a lone staffer sweeps in even
    strokes,
changing the dust for a brand-new day.

Two women in white uniforms stand under the bus sign,
sharing a Grande cup between them.

Laborers in jeans and dark shirts pace the plaza sidewalk,
ambling for opportunity when a truck stops. A hand
from the truck's window, gestures for three.

Across the plaza, wood planks cross out windows,
where ghosts of commerce dig deep in dusty buildings.

St. Augustine Church stands in patient silence,
waiting for its doors to reopen to the faithful.

On this breezy August morning, sensational headlines
and travel warnings lift away. In this moment,
Laredo has a chance to be reborn, if not today, tomorrow.

—Diane Gonzales Bertrand

THE KENTUCKY CLUB, JUAREZ

the margarita was born
just across the Santa Fe bridge

where Jack Dempsey stumbled out on all fours
where Marilyn celebrated her last divorce
where mescal still masks the thirst of desire

and lust lights their cigarettes

where Chapo moves cocaine
and young soldiers, rifles over their shoulders
languish on the corner

where the jukebox
like the killing never wants to stop

—*Jerry Bradley*

BOYS' TOWN, CIUDAD ACUÑA

like the doors at the Palacio de Oro
the women here swing both ways
and gather like schoolgirls
in corner booths to gossip about boys

it's the same at the Durango
where Blandina dispenses her penny-candy *besitos*
to Texans in stenciled belts
and embroidered shirts

they kiss back, feel her soft *chichis*

for a dollar Adelita would lick the spit
off a dog's lips and for twenty
turn puppy love dog-style

but the *Extranjero* is best for those
on benders, between marriages,
or amid a bad one

pay a boy to watch the car
but keep running money in the trunk
just in case

and when you pull out
drunk but dissatisfied
ignore the Indios
selling chiclets and beads

and the street dogs
that circle the taco cart
like hyenas

convince yourself
you're not one of them
not just another mongrel
trying to outlast
a bottom-of-the-bottle life

then beat it back to Del Rio
disregarding the fallen night,
the dead dove twisting in your grill

—*Jerry Bradley*

LA LLORONA TRANSFORMS
FROM WOMAN TO SNAKE,
CONSIDERING A LOVER'S BETRAYAL

His sickness compares to mine?
Releasing children to a stream
is nothing. They drifted off,
disappeared, barely
rippling the watercourse. I slipped
into the Hands of God
two shiny pesos.

I had
nothing to do
with his purchasing
a whore's favors.
I was wet.
He longed
for a *puta*.

He accreted his lies
down to rings
on a rattlesnake's tail.

He saddled his horse.
I snapped his clothes
in his face,
lunged at his mount
with a pitchfork's fangs,

with my arm's
overlapping scales.

My eyes' transparent
lids unblinking,

tongue split
as the chicken eggs
I unhinged my jaw
to swallow,

shells spit,
those shucked
husks of
demon
seed.

—Paul David Adkins

SANTA MUERTE DRIVES A WHITE ESCALADE

Transparent skin stretched over hollows
mirrored sunglasses conceal. Tinted

windshields. Narco-corridos boom
music on shattered speakers

only she can hear. *Santa Muerte* drag
races *sola* through strings of red

Christmas lights, spinning tinsel
tires, picking up hitchhikers, *cholas,*

soldiers, lawyers, babies, *viejas,*
vatos, maquileras y Jésus

Malverde at the S-Mart in Anapra,
and souls twinkling in the valley

below. Cristo Rey. *Políticos y altos*
jefes tambien tienen su altar. La Muerte

swerves between *ruteras,* past checkpoints,
federales and empty torta stands. *La Patrona*

está en todos lados. Over mountains
to the minefields. What remains

of old war games. Unexploded earth. Door
handles rattle. Reaching for power

locks, she accelerates. Sonic bang
into searchlights. Beaming.

—*Abigail Carl-Klassen*

WHEN THE GHOSTS STAY

You have terror and I have tears.
In this cruel way, we are for each other.

We are at war. You always win.
But I do not go away.

You shoot me again. Again, I do not go away.
You shoot with bullets, but you have nothing else.

I fight back. I shoot you
With fragments of childhood, where you played the hero.

I shoot you with memories of your mother
And your little sister, Maritza.

I shoot you with spring in the rolling mountains
And the taste of plantain bananas and sugar.

You do not fall down dead—
You can kill me, where all I can do

Is hold up the mirror of remembering to you—
The mirror of everything you have done.

You set fire to me with gasoline.
I set fire to you with the memory of your first love.

You cut my hands off. I cut your hands off
With the way you saw them disappear

When he was diving into the warm water of the lake,
The summer of swimming with your brother.

Do you remember the names of the left-for-dead?
The damaged, the hounded, the hurt?

Do you remember my name?

Your fist is hard.
My name is crying.

You strike a match.
My name is cringe.

You lift your foot.
My name is pain.

You wake up.
My name is closed eyes.

Your smile mimics the size of the opening
On the side of a head, a crude opening

That a mean needle will stitch up tonight.
Your arm laughs at me with its muscle.

All this. All these tears you have made,
This water you have found in the desert,

All this blood you have drawn
From the bodies of so many who needed it.

You win. You have always won.
All I can do is not go away.

Not go away is my name.

—Alberto Ríos

GLOSSARY

altos jefes	big-time bosses
los ancianos	the old people
Anapra	poor neighborhood in Juarez that lies directly across the border at El Paso
a pie	on foot
Arch at Kabah	the gateway to the sacbe, or causeway, linking Kabah, one of the ancient Mayan cities to Uxmal. On the interior of the arch at Kabah is painted a red hand. On the matching gate at Uxmal, approximately 8 miles away, is painted a blue hand. The Mayan word Kabah means "strong hand" or "skilled hand."
baile	a dance
besitos	little kisses
bolillo	a baked plain roll or bun of white flour, sometimes used as a nickname for Anglo Americans
bruja	witch (female)

el cadejo	the Aztec canine equivalent to Cerberus, guard dog to the underworld.
café	coffee
calle	street
cambio de piel	change of skin
camiones	trucks
carne	beef
una casa azul	a blue house
Cenote Sagrada	The Sacred Well is a Mayan limestone sinkhole found at the pre-Columbian site of Chichén Itzá in the northern Yucatan peninsula. The well was used for ritual purposes including human sacrifice to appease the Mayan rain god, Chaac.
cerveza fria	cold beer
chico	little boy
Chipinque	rock formation atop a foothill of the Sierra Madre
cholas	homegirls
concursos	TV game shows
corazón	heart
corridos	bullfights
Cristo Rey	Christ the King, a mountain that borders the Anapra neighborhood
curandera	a folk healer (female)

depósito	convenience store
dos Laredos	the two Laredos
español	the Spanish language
estoque	sword
extranjero	the foreigner, or in some cases, the stranger
federales	Mexican federal police
gringo	a disparaging term for a foreigner, especially an American
guajira	a peasant woman
Huastec	indigenous Mesoamericans who emigrated from the Yucatan Peninsula millennia ago to settle in northern Mexico
Isla de la Piedra	a peninsula in Mazatlán that means "Island of Stone"
Jesús Malverde	folklore hero in Mexican state of Sinaloa, particularly to narco-traffickers
Ladinos	a group of metizo peoples in the Americas
La Malinche	the indigenous Aztec woman who aided Hernán Cortés in the conquest of the Aztec Empire
los manos de la campaña	the hands of the companion (female)
maquileras	factory workers (female)
mariposa monarca	Monarch butterfly
mesón	an inn

milagros	literally, miracles. Also the name for small metal icons representing prayers answered or prayers requested.
¡Mira!	Look!
las monjas	the nuns
La Muerte	Death
narco-corridos	songs celebrating narco-traffickers
mis niños	my boys, my small children (male)
niñas	girls
Nopalli	the Nahuatl word for a cactus bearing large, edible fleshy pads on which the cochineal insect, which gave a red dye, was raised.
norteamericana	North American (female)
noticias	the news
pan dulce	sweet bread
La Patrona	a female employer, also used in reference to female saints
pelo	hair
personas	persons
piloncillo	Mexican brown sugar hardened into cones
Playa Norte	North Beach, a beach in Mazatlán
políticos	politicians
por la libre	down the freeway
posada	inn

pulque	an alcoholic beverage made from the fermented sap of the maguey plant
puta	whore
¡que linda güerita!	What a pretty little blonde girl!
Río del Oro	river of gold
rutera	a bus painted with a numbered route
Santa Muerte	Saint Death
santo	saint, and may also refer to statues or wooden carvings of saints
sierra	mountain range
sola	alone (female)
El Tajín	a pre-Columbian archaeological site in southern Mexico. Among many other startling examples of cultural architecture, several ball courts have been excavated there.
también	also
Tehuanas	women of the municipality of Tehuantepec, in the southern Mexican state of Oaxaca. Their matriarchal society inspired painter Frida Kahlo to don the distinctive dress of the Tehuana in many of her paintings.
Templo Mayor	one of the Aztec main temples in Tenochtitlán
el tendero	the shopkeeper (male)
Tenochtitlán	Aztec city-state founded in 1325 on an island in the middle of Lake Texcoco in the Valley of Mexico

tienda de hierbas espirituales	shop of spiritual herbs
todos lados	in all places, on all sides
topes	speed bumps
torera	a bullfighter (female)
torta	sandwich popular in Mexico and other Latin American countries
telenovela	a soap opera
vaquero	cowboy
vatos	homeboys
viejo/a	old man/woman
Xolotl	the Aztec god associated both with lightning and death.

STATEMENTS ABOUT CONTRIBUTORS' RELATIONSHIPS WITH MEXICO

Paul David Adkins
Though I have visited Mexico's border town of Nogales, it is the mythic quality of the culture which most strongly attracts me. From the legends of La Llorona and El Duende to Pancho Villa's invasion of the United States, Mexico has always held for me a mysterious, haunting quality.

Diana Anhalt
In 1950 my parents left the United States during the McCarthy era and resided in Mexico, a country which accepted many political expatriates. They left, but I remained for 60 years until I moved to Atlanta, GA three years ago and, since then, all I've been able to write about is Mexico.

José Angel Araguz
My relationship to Mexico is one of leaving and looking back: my mother left my father in Matamoros and crossed the river into Texas to raise me, but would wonder aloud about him. My father, his mother, my mother's father – each has died in my lifetime in Matamoros. My childhood was visits to Mexico, until the drug trafficking made travel dangerous, and so I look back in my writings at what is left in those visits.

Jack B. Bedell
Since my earliest contact with Mayan and Aztec cultures in grade school, I've been entranced by Mexico's diverse and mysterious history. While my main connections might come from textbooks

and art, my respect for the soul of the country, and the legacy it has left western civilization, is profound.

Diane Gonzales Bertrand
I've genuflected to the beauty in Mexico City and San Miguel de Allende, kissed family in Monterrey, and shivered under the mistrust and suspicion of the border towns of Laredo and Progreso. Remaining hopeful, I pray for hospitality and safety to guide me back to a country that remains radiant in my deepest memories.

Alan Birkelbach
I was a child of the 1960s in Texas. There were whites, Mexicans, negroes—but everything was distinct and part of a caste system that went back generations. Today, surrounded by scores of restaurants serving bland, homogeneous, cultural food, I'm not sure we're better off.

David Bowles
I come from a family with deep Mexican-American and Southern roots, and the mingling of those cultural traditions has shaped me. Most of my life has been spent in the Rio Grande Valley of South Texas, crisscrossing the border for family and cultural reasons. I married a woman from Monterrey, Nuevo León, and living in/ travelling to different areas of Mexico with her strengthened my connections to that country until it felt like a second home.

Jerry Bradley
Mexico is like an old girlfriend: you want the best for her but are wary of getting too close. No matter how charming and alluring she seems, she is always capable of turning on you and breaking your heart.

Abigail Carl-Klassen
I worked in the non-profit/social services sector in the El Paso/ Juarez border region for several years before becoming an English instructor at the El Paso Community College and the University of Texas at El Paso. I also worked alongside community development organizations in Mexico City.

Sherry Craven
Mexico was a time and a place of warm sun, cool drinks, quiet roads rising into green woods, houses fenced by ocotillo and welcoming people. A land of the fragrances of the open markets,

taste of fresh fruits, sounds of maracas, a musical language, and a rich folklore. Cities were vibrant and most of all–safe. A land of an easy pace, bougainvillea colors, guitar music, street tamales, and fine restaurant paella.

Carolyn Dahl
My relationship to Mexico was simple at first: visiting Mayan ruins in thick jungles, buying embroidered huipils, listening to mariachi bands, and standing in awe before famous murals. Now, my memories are overlaid with new complexities: development, violence, and the van loads of immigrants seeking a better life in our country, just as busloads of tourists used to flood their country.

Jim Daniels
I was double majoring in Spanish at Alma College, a small school in Michigan, when they announced a one-month intensive course in Mexico. My writing teacher urged me to go. I didn't have the money, but he convinced the financial aid guy to give me a loan. I had never been on an airplane before—my first big adventure in life. I had grown up in a factory town near Detroit, so arriving in Mexico was the equivalent of going from black-and-white TV to color—that trip changed my entire approach to life. To me, Mexico represented an opening up to the larger world.

Maureen Tolman Flannery has traveled extensively in Mexico, both as a child and with her husband and children who have hosted numerous Mexican young adults learning English. The couple's four children are fluent in Spanish and have built upon a love of the culture.

James Hoggard has taught in several institutions in Mexico, both in Chihuahua and in San Miguel de Allende. In both places his work there, and the friendships he made, have had a powerful effect on him; and friendships he made in several places have remained current, certainly in spirit. On the other hand, some violent events that have touched him personally have kept him away from the country; and from his point of view that spells great loss.

Ann Howells
Raised on the East Coast and moving to Texas after beginning my family, I found both the Texan and Mexican cultures colorful and exciting. I travel to Mexico, mostly the border towns, whenever

I have an opportunity. I love the language, the architecture, the music, the food and the people.

Lois P. Jones
Mexico is a faithful lover. She wears the same perfume: roasted cinnamon, grilled gorditas. She awakens me to the sound of church bells like cast-iron pans and the rooster outside my window. She seeps through the rusted pipes of my shower and breathes her simple grace. Wraps around me like the frayed cotton towels at *Posada de las Monjas*. There is nothing I could want for when I am there except the impossible. Never to leave.

Kate Kingston returns to Mexico every January for the San Miguel Poetry Week, jump-starting her new year with poetry and friends while immersing herself in the complex culture that is Mexico.

AM Krohn's affection for Mexico comes from living on the border during the first decades of his life and his extensive travels in the country.

Peter Ludwin
In addition to participating in the San Miguel Poetry Week for 12 years, I have traveled extensively in Mexico because I love the warmth of its people, the Spanish language, the food and the indigenous influence. In particular, I am familiar with parts of the Sierra Tarahumara in Chihuahua, Mazatlán, the state of Guanajuato, parts of Michoacan and Oaxaca. Due to my 9 winters in the Texas Big Bend, I also came to love the hardscrabble village of Boquillas in the state of Coahuila.

Tony Mares
Mexico was in the beans, chile, and tortillas I ate as a child. Mexico was in the Spanish language, the religious beliefs and practices of my family, and our travels back and forth to Ciudad Juárez, and later, in the images of Villa and Zapata on my bedroom wall. My grandmother would turn an image of a saint backwards if it did not produce some good and Mexico is that saint still often sadly standing backwards, and yes, it is time to turn that saint around to face the future once again.

Kathleen Markowitz
In 1980 the pre-Columbian archaeological site, Chichén Itzá had yet to be designated as a World Cultural Heritage Site, and it

was not prohibited to climb the steep staircase of the pyramid, El Castillo. I was able to ascend only thirty of its ninety-one smooth slippery steps. I also became attentive to the sacred *descantos* or roadside shrines where some believe the place where a soul left the body is marked.

Janet McCann
My most extensive connection with Mexico was my participation in the Faculty Seminar Abroad, in which we visited universities all around Mexico for the purpose of initiating mutual projects. It was an intense experience, designed to teach us history and culture as well as to help us make friends. I did establish wonderful working friendships with colleagues, which still exist.

Celeste Guzmán Mendoza an eighth-generation Tejana, is a Mexican American. Her maternal grandfather was born and raised in Mexico, and fled his family's hacienda in Nuevo León during Mexico's revolution. Her maternal grandmother's ancestors fought in the Battle of San Jacinto, gaining Texas' independence from Mexico. Raised on her family's oral histories as well as the *hacendado* culture of northern Mexico, Mendoza focuses her writing about Mexico on the people and the landscape.

karla k. morton
Mexico has always been that dark-headed man at the end of the bar—the steamy one with the beer. Sometimes he gives me that look, and I can't help but journey his way, my purse packed with lip gloss, and a low-cut sundress bought just for him.

For Erin O'Luanaigh, the allure of Mexico took hold in childhood, when her grandparents sent daily postcards from their travels through the country's remotest villages. Her love of Mexican culture has made the art of the region a particular interest, especially the works of Mexico's most famous daughter, Frida Kahlo.

Carol Coffee Reposa
My love for Mexico reaches back to my earliest years. I was born on the California-Baja border. As a young adult, I made exuberant trips to Saltillo, Zacatecas, Guadalajara, and Mazatlán. Then, in 2005, I received a Fulbright-Hays Fellowship for study in Chiapas, Oaxaca, and Mexico City, an experience that changed my life.

Jan Seale
I have lived in South Texas on the border for all of my adult life and have written much about the bi-cultural and natural environment. It is a very special place, with an exoticism of peoples, plants, and animals not found anywhere else in the U.S. Although our lives have been drastically diminished due to narco-violence, I cling to the hope that someday there will again be easy passage among our peoples.

Martha Serpas
When I was a student in Houston, I used my vacation time to explore Mexico: first, all over Quintana Roo, then Mexico City and Puebla. I drove down the Baja peninsula with friends, camping along those stunning nooks with no one for miles around. The groundedness and faith of the friends I made there, the vast landscape of all terrains, kept me returning.

Loueva Smith
In 1992 I spent several months in Mercedes, Texas at the home of a friend. We crossed the Rio Grande Bridge on foot to visit Flores, Mexico several times a week. We went in search of treats: mangoes and ice cream, curious skulls, reproductions of Aztec gods, and, most especially, Catholic Churches with long tables lit with quivering candles, heat waves shimmering in the darkened room seeming to ache with longing for help. The memory of it saturates me still.

Seth Strickland
My relationship with Mexico is but tenuous. Having never been, I had the unique privilege nonetheless of teaching its history to students who had been. As a native of the U.S., Mexico is always on my mind, and the discouragement I feel due to the drug violence must only be surpassed by that felt by the long-suffering citizens of Mexico. In that, as in so many things, we share a common hope for a better future.

Sandi Stromberg
My high-school Spanish teacher assigned readings from Jorge Luis Borges, Federico Garcia Lorca, Pablo Neruda, and others. These writers excited my mind. When the opportunity arose to explore Mexico, I reveled in my time there and discovered Carlos Fuentes.

Melissa Studdard
Having grown up in Texas, I've enjoyed a long and personal relationship with Mexican culture, but the Mexico of this poem is of another time altogether, the WWII era, in which Mexico accepted a stream of European émigrés, many of whom were surrealists.

Larry D. Thomas has long enjoyed visiting Mexico, especially Mexico City and Monterrey. Among the many things he loves in Mexico City are its incomparable murals and the Blue House of Frida Kahlo and Diego Rivera.

C. Derick Varn
My relationship to Mexico is both complicated and not. I live in Torreón, Coahuila, and have for the past year. I am not Latino, and I do not speak for Mexico's culture. I, however, have learned to begrudging love Mexico. I teach the children of the privileged, and even they have been traumatized by recent narco-cartel violence. Yet the community has been incredibly kind to me, and open in a way that has made me very empathetic to Mexico's precarious beauty.

Germaine Welch
All my life have I played along the Border: Tijuana, Matamoras, Nuevo Laredo, Juárez. My children's first train ride was from Laredo to Mexico City where we went to museums, rode buses, bought art, climbed the steps of Teotihuacan. Mexico has been both playground and school where I and my children could learn the value of cultural diversity.

Patrick Allen Wright
I lived in Hidalgo County, Texas from January 1988 through the summer of 1995. I visited extensively the entire Rio Grande Valley from Brownsville to Laredo. Also, I journeyed into Mexico for lengthy visits.

Rebecca Young Eun Yook
I went to Tizimin in 2003 with my parents' church. In broken Spanish, we asked people to accept Jesus into their hearts. On our last day, we went to Chichén Itzá and I saw a boy fall from one of the temples. It sounded like a watermelon breaking. Outside of this experience, my relationship with Mexico has been through her artists—Frida's battles with her doctors, her lovers and her selves bring out the fighter and creator in me.

CONTRIBUTORS' BIOGRAPHIES

Paul David Adkins lives in New York and works as a counselor. He served in the US Army for 21 years. He holds degrees from Washington University and Mercer University. He has poetry chapbooks published through Blood Pudding, Kind of a Hurricane, and Yellow Jacket Presses.

Diana Anhalt is the author of *A Gathering of Fugitives* (Archer Books), three chapbooks, including *Second Skin* (Future Cycle) and *Lives of Straw* (Finishing Line Press), and of essays, short stories and book reviews in both English and Spanish. Her writing has received awards from Passager, The Writers Place, Common Ground, Litchfield Review and Frith Press.

José Angel Araguz, author of the chapbooks *The Wall* (Tiger's Eye Press), *Naos* (Right Hand Pointing), and *Corpus Christi Octaves* (Flutter Press), is a CantoMundo fellow and has had poems recently in *Barrow Street*, *RHINO*, *Hanging Loose* and *Poet Lore*. He is presently pursuing a Ph.D. in Creative Writing at the University of Cincinnati.

Jack B. Bedell is Professor of English and Coordinator of Creative Writing at Southeastern Louisiana University where he also edits *Louisiana Literature* and directs the Louisiana Literature Press. His latest collections are *Bone-Hollow, True: New & Selected Poems, Call & Response, Come Rain, Come Shine, What Passes for Love* and *At the Bonehouse*, all published by Texas Review Press.

Diane Gonzales Bertrand is the Writer-in-Residence at St. Mary's University in San Antonio, TX, teaching English Composition and Creative Writing. Her poems have been published in *The Texas Poetry Calendar, VIA Poetry on the Move*, and *Concho River Review. Dawn Flower* (Pecan Grove Press, 2013) is her debut poetry collection. She also writes books for children and teens.

Alan Birkelbach, a native Texan, is the 2005 Poet Laureate of Texas. His work has appeared in journals, such as *Grasslands Review, Borderlands, The Langdon Review*, and *Concho River Review*, and anthologies. He is member of The Texas Institute of Letters and the Academy of American Poets. He has nine collections of poetry.

David Bowles is author of several books, including *Shattering and Bricolage, The Seed, Mexican Bestiary*, and *Flower, Song, Dance: Aztec and Mayan Poetry*, which was awarded the 2014 Soeurette Diehl Frasier Award for Best Translation. His work has appeared in journals, including *Translation Review, Concho River Review, Huizache, Red River Review, Ilya's Honey, James Gunn's Ad Astra*, and *BorderSenses*.

Jerry Bradley is Professor of English at Lamar University. He is the author of three volumes of poetry: *Simple Versions of Disaster, The Importance of Elsewhere*, and *Crownfeathers and Effigies*. A member of the Texas Institute of Letters, he is poetry editor of *Concho River Review*. His poetry has appeared in *New England Review, Modern Poetry Studies, Poetry Magazine*, and *Southern Humanities Review*.

Agustín Cadena was born in the Valle de Mezquital, Hidalgo, Mexico. For several years Cadena has been living in Hungary, where he is a professor at the University of Debrecen. Author of more than twenty books, including the poetry collection, *Cacería de Brujas*, Cadena writes in multiple genres, including the novel, screenplay, short story, poem, essay, and children's literature.

Abigail Carl-Klassen's work has appeared or is forthcoming in *Cimarron Review, Guernica*, and *Huizache*, among others and is anthologized in *New Border Voices* (Texas A&M University Press). She earned an MFA from the University of Texas El Paso's Bilingual Creative Writing Program and taught at El Paso Community College and the University of Texas at El Paso.

Sarah Cortez is a Councilor of the Texas Institute of Letters and graduate of Rice University. Winner of the PEN Texas Literary Award in poetry, she has two collections of poetry, one memoir and has edited seven anthologies. Her most recent is *Our Lost Border: Essays on Life amid the Narco-Violence*, winner of a Southwest Book Award and an International Latino Book Award. She was recently named to the 2014-16 Texas Commission of the Arts Touring Roster.

Sherry Craven taught high school Spanish and college English at Midland College and West Texas A&M. She is published in *Amarillo Bay, New Texas, Two Southwests, The Witness, Windhover, descant, The Langdon Review, RiverSedge, The Texas Review, Concho River Review, Suddenly, Texas Poetry 2, Quotable Texas Women,* and *Writing on the Wind.* She won the Conference of College Teachers of English 2005 poetry award and published a poetry collection entitled *Standing by the Window.*

Carolyn Dahl's essays and poems have been published in twenty-five anthologies, including *Women On Poetry, Beyond Forgetting,* and literary journals such as *Copper Nickel, Camas, Hawai'i Review,* and *Colere.* She was a PEN Texas finalist in nonfiction, and author of *Transforming Fabric* (F&W Media) & *Natural Impressions* (Watson-Guptill), and co-author of *The Painted Door Opened: Poetry and Art.*

Jim Daniels' fourteenth book of poems, *Birth Marks*, was published by BOA Editions in 2013 and was selected as a Michigan Notable Book, winner of the Milton Kessler Poetry Book Award, and received the Gold Medal in Poetry in the Independent Publishers Book Awards. His fifth book of short fiction, *Eight Mile High*, was published by Michigan State University Press in 2014. A native of Detroit, Daniels is the Thomas Stockham Baker University Professor of English at Carnegie Mellon University.

Margo Davis' recent journal publications include *Agave Magazine, A Clean, Well-Lighted Place* and *The Sow's Ear Poetry Review.* Anthologies include *Houston Poetry Fest, Texas Poetry Calendar, Lifting the Sky,* and *Through a Distant Lens: Travel Poems.*

Martín Espada has published more than fifteen books. His latest collection of poems, *The Trouble Ball* (Norton), received the Milt Kessler Award, a Massachusetts Book Award and an International Latino Book Award. A previous collection, *The Republic of Poetry*

(Norton) was a finalist for the Pulitzer Prize. The recipient of a Guggenheim Fellowship and the Shelley Memorial Award, Espada teaches at the University of Massachusetts-Amherst.

Maureen Tolman Flannery is the author of seven books of poetry, including *Tunnel into Morning, Destiny Whispers to the Beloved,* Pulitzer Prize-nominated *Ancestors in the Landscape* and *Secret of the Rising Up: Poems of Mexico.* She is recipient of an Illinois Arts Award, several Pushcart Prize nominations, and first place in national contests. More than five hundred of her poems have been published in anthologies, journals, and literary reviews.

James Hoggard, The Perkins—Prothro Distinguished Professor of English, Emeritus at Midwestern State University in Wichita Falls, Texas is the author of more than 20 books, including novels, collections of stories, poems, personal essays, and literary translations. Seven of his plays have been produced. The winner of numerous awards for his writing, he was recently named a Fellow of the Texas Institute of Letters. Work of his has been published in the *Harvard Review, Southwest Review*, and numerous other places.

Ann Howells' work appears in *Calyx, Crannog, Little Patuxent Review, Magma, Sentence and Spillway* among many others. She edits *Illya's Honey.* Her chapbooks are: *Black Crow in Flight* and *Rosebud Diaries.* She has won first place in poetry contests and has been twice nominated for a Pushcart Prize.

Elizabeth Humber, a student at St. Agnes Academy, has won two statewide poetry contests at a convention for Junior Beta Club, an honors society. She has won the St. Agnes' annual Library Poetry Contest.

Lois P. Jones is a host of L.A. radio's "Poet's Café." Some publications include *Tupelo Quarterly, Narrative Magazine, The Warwick Review*, and *American Poetry Journal. New Yorker* staff writer Dana Goodyear selected "Ouija" as Poem of the Year (2010). Jones won the 2012 *Tiferet* Prize and is featured in *The Tiferet Talk Interviews* with Robert Pinsky. She is Poetry Editor of *Kyoto Journal.*

Kate Kingston has published two books of poetry, *History of Grey*, a runner-up in the 2013 Main Street Rag Poetry Book Award and *Shaking the Kaleidoscope*, a finalist in the 2011 Idaho Prize for

Poetry. She is the recipient of the W.D Snodgrass Award for Poetic Endeavor and Excellence, the Ruth Stone Prize, and the Atlanta Review International Publication Prize.

AM Krohn is originally from El Paso. His last public appearance as a writer was at the Houston Poetry Fest in 1997 when he was the featured poet. He lives, works and writes in Houston, Texas.

Peter Ludwin is the recipient of a Literary Fellowship from Artist Trust. His most recent book, *Rumors of Fallible Gods*, was twice a finalist for the Gival Press Poetry Prize. For twelve years he has been a participant in the San Miguel Poetry Week in Mexico. His work has appeared in *Crab Orchard Review*, *Nimrod*, *Prairie Schooner* and *Spillway*, among other journals.

Tony Mares' recent poetry books are *Astonishing Light* (University of New Mexico Press, 2010); *Río Del Corazón*, (Voices of the American Land, 2010); translations of the Spanish poet Ángel González, *Casi Toda la Música y otros poemas/Almost All the Music and Other Poems* (Wings Press, 2007). His poems appear in over 23 reviews and anthologies. He has a Ph.D. in Modern European History from the University of New Mexico.

Paul Mariani, the University Professor of English at Boston College, is the author of seven volumes of poetry, most recently *Epitaphs for the Journey* (Cascade, 2012). He has published biographies of William Carlos Williams, Hart Crane, John Berryman, Robert Lowell, Gerard Manley Hopkins; his life of Wallace Stevens, *The Whole Harmonium*, will be published by Simon & Schuster next August.

Kathleen Markowitz is the recipient of the Leslie Shiel Endowed Fellowship in Creative Writing established through the Visual Arts Center of Richmond, Virginia, and the Paul and Eileen Mariani Fellowship for Poets at *Image Journal*. Her work has been published in *Crab Creek Review* and *Hawaii Pacific Review*. Her work received a first place award in the 2009 National Poetry Competition sponsored by the Poetry Society of Virginia.

C.M. Mayo is the author of *Metaphysical Odyssey Into the Mexican Revolution: Francisco I. Madero and His Secret Book, Spiritist Manual*; the novel *The Last Prince of the Mexican Empire*, which was a Library Journal Best Book 2009, and *Sky Over El*

Nido: Stories, which won the Flannery O'Connor Award, all three translated into Spanish by Agustín Cadena. Mayo has translated stories by Cadena, one of which appears in her collection *Mexico: A Traveler's Literary Companion*.

Janet McCann has been published in journals including *Kansas Quarterly, Parnassus, Nimrod, Sou'wester, Christian Century, New York Quarterly, Tendril*, and *McCall's*. She has three books and six chapbooks. A 1989 NEA Creative Writing Fellowship winner, she is currently Professor of English at A&M. Her most recent poetry book is *The Crone at the Casino* (Lamar University Press, 2013).

Celeste Guzmán Mendoza writes poetry, plays, and essays. Her debut poetry book, *Beneath the Halo*, was published by Wings Press in 2013. Her second, *Coming in Waves*, is forthcoming in 2015. She is co-director and a co-founder of CantoMundo, a workshop for Latina/o poets, and has participated in the Macondo Writers Workshop.

karla k. morton, the 2010 Texas Poet Laureate, is a Councilor of the Texas Institute of Letters and a graduate of Texas A&M University. Described as "one of the most adventurous voices in American poetry," she's a Betsy Colquitt Award Winner, twice an Indie National Book Award Winner, the recipient of the Writer-in-Residency E2C Grant, and the author of nine collections of poetry.

Erin O'Luanaigh is a jazz vocalist and music teacher from Cheshire, Connecticut. She is a recent graduate of Hillsdale College in Michigan, where she received the Barnes Award for Excellence in Poetry in 2012. Her poetry and prose have previously appeared in *Commonweal*, the *National Catholic Register*, and *Pilgrim*.

Carol Coffee Reposa's poems, essays and articles have appeared in *The Atlanta Review, Southwestern American Literature, The Valparaiso Review, The Evansville Review*, and other journals and anthologies. Author of four books of poetry, she has received three Pushcart Prize nominations, along with three Fulbright-Hays Fellowships, and twice been short-listed for Texas Poet Laureate. She now serves as poetry editor of *Voices de la Luna*.

Alberto Ríos is Arizona's first state poet laureate and a Regents' Professor at Arizona State University and the Katharine C. Turner

Endowed Chair in English. He is the author of ten books and chapbooks of poetry, three collections of short stories, and a memoir. His books of poems include, most recently, *The Dangerous Shirt*, along with *The Theater of Night*, winner of the 2007 PEN/ Beyond Margins Award. His awards include fellowships from the Guggenheim Foundation and the National Endowment from the Arts.

Jan Seale, the 2012 Texas Poet Laureate, lives seven miles from the Texas-Mexico border in the Lower Rio Grande Valley. Her poems are collected in nine volumes: *Bonds, Sharing the House, Believing is Seeing, The Yin of It, Valley Ark, The Wonder Is, Nape, Jan Seale: New and Selected Poems*, and *The Parkinson Poems*.

Martha Serpas' three collections of poetry are *Côte Blanche, The Dirty Side of the Storm* and *The Diener*. Her work has appeared in *The New Yorker, The Nation, Image*, and *Southwest Review*. Active in efforts to restore Louisiana's wetlands, she co-produced *Veins in the Gulf*, a documentary about coastal erosion. She teaches in the Creative Writing Program at the University of Houston and serves as a hospital trauma chaplain.

Loueva Smith's poetry has been published in *DoubleTake, The Texas Review, The Louisiana Review, Pearl, Kalliope*, and *Nerve Cowboy*. Her plays, *Bruna Bunny and Baby Girl*, and *Tenderina*, have been staged at The Frenetic Theater in Houston, Texas.

Seth Strickland's publications include poems published in *The Tower Light*, which he later edited. He was involved in writing at Hillsdale College where he received his undergraduate degree in English and in Classical Studies. He will continue his education in English Literature this fall at Saint Louis University.

Sandi Stromberg has been nominated for a Pushcart Prize, been published in seven Houston Poetry Fest anthologies, and placed in both San Antonio and Dallas Poets Community contests. Her poems have appeared in *Borderlands, Illya's Honey, Improbable Worlds, The Weight of Addition, TimeSlice, Texas Poetry Calendars, Colere*, as well as other journals and anthologies.

Melissa Studdard is the author of the bestselling novel, *Six Weeks to Yehidah* and other books. She has received numerous awards, including the Forward National Literature Award and the International Book Award. Her first poetry collection, *I Ate the Cosmos for Breakfast*, is forthcoming (fall, 2014). She reviews and edits for several journals and is a host for *Tiferet Talk* radio.

Larry D. Thomas, the 2008 Texas Poet Laureate, has received several awards for his poetry, including two Texas Review Poetry Prizes (2001 and 2004), the 2003 Western Heritage Wrangler Award and the 2004 Violet Crown Book Award. His *New and Selected Poems* (TCU Press, 2008) was a semi-finalist for the National Book Award.

C. Derick Varn is a poet, teacher, and theorist. He currently edits for Former People. He has a MFA in Poetry from Georgia College and State University where he was assistant editor for *Arts and Letters: A Journal of Contemporary Arts*. He won the Frankeye Davis Mayes/Academy of American Poets Prize in 2003; his poetry has appeared at *Writing Disorder, JMWW, Xenith, Piriene's Fountain*, and elsewhere.

Randall Watson is the author of *The Sleep Accusations*, 2003/04 recipient of the Blue Lynx Prize and published by Eastern Washington University Press, *Las Delaciones del Sueño*, published by La Universidad Veracruzana in Mexico, and *Petals*, winner of the 2007/08 Quarterly West Novella Competition. He edited *The Weight of Addition: An Anthology of Texas Poetry* for Mutabilis Press.

Germaine Welch lives in Houston, TX and has a Ph.D. in Anthropology from Rice University. Her poetry has been published in *The Lineup: Poems on Crime*.

Patrick Allen Wright was born in Beaumont, Texas and graduated in 1984 with forty-five publications, ten awards, and the first creative writing Master's thesis of poems at Lamar University. He has published poems and an essay in *Langdon Review of the Arts*, and poems in several Texas Poetry Calendars.

Rebecca Young Eun Yook was born in South Korea. She earned a degree from Rutgers University and currently lives in New Jersey. She writes poems to experience naked melody and truth. Rebecca is also a singer.